GOD HELP

ALL LITTLE CHILDREN

READ, WRITE and SPELL

GOD HELP

ALL LITTLE CHILDREN

READ, WRITE and SPELL

By

Ian Duck

ISBN: 1-58820-179-1

1stBooks - rev 9/26/00

TABLE OF CONTENTS

Dedication...vii

Chapter I
The Problem Of The English Language. 3

Chapter II
The Phonics Wars. 13

Chapter III
Benjamin Franklin's Phonics...25

Chapter IV
Elements Of Modular English. 45

Chapter V
Modular English In The Classics..73

Chapter VI
Modular English In Expository Prose...87

Chapter VII
Modular English: Unique? Not Exactly..................................103

Chapter VIII
Modular English: Ebonics? Gullah?...119

Chapter IX
Education For A Changing World. 135

Chapter X
Post-Traumatic Stress Disorder From Spelling? 150

Chapter XI
Implementation Of Modular English Reform...........................163

DEDICATION

I dedicate this book and the whole concept of Modular English to my son **Eric**. My thinking about reform of written English began thirty years ago in a letter to the editor of the Houston Post, prompted by the difficulties Eric was experiencing with grade school spelling. Eric is now a college graduate, he has survived wonderful adventures on worldwide geophysical explorations, he is a talented photographer, raconteur, chess and tennis player, computer expert, financial adviser, a better husband and father than I was, and works as a land development surveyor. He reads widely with particular interest in geography and world politics. He is my antithesis in that he is sweet, gentle and even tempered. I have never heard him utter an angry or profane or blasphemous word nor even a harsh or ill-considered opinion.

I also dedicate this book to **Nicholas** , a remarkable 10-year old 4th-grade student at Houston's McGregor Elementary School, an inner-city magnet school for science and music. I happened upon Nicholas when I volunteered as a community tutor. I have never inquired how or why I was assigned to Nicholas, but getting to know him has been a profound learning experience for me. As far as I can tell, apart from an almost pathological reticence, he has no faults. He has no difficulty learning whatever is asked of him. What I have done for him I can say is not much, and nothing he wouldn't have survived quite nicely without. We work at guessing the answers before reading the assignments; then searching the reading assignment for specific answers. Watching him do arithmetic in his head is tremendous fun: he closes his eyes, scrunches up his mouth, and slowly, ever so slowly, the answers come out correctly. We approach arithmetic problems by estimating the answer; by adding or multiplying from left to right; by making approximations. None of these are concepts I was explicitly acquainted with before college.

What Nicholas has done for me is another question. First of all, I quite unabashedly have loved him from the first time I met

vii

him. It was some months -- we only meet one hour a week -- before I was able to see him as a real person and his flaws truly are very minor. Like Eric, he is a completely gentle person. All the children at McGregor are unbelievably sweet and well behaved. Why this is true I can't say. Even bulky little boys who are already being trained by their fathers as football and basketball players are completely gentle in word and deed. McGregor is a very special place, so it's not right to generalize about all little Black 4th-graders from the few I have met. Nonetheless, these are the most beautiful and exemplary children it is possible to imagine. Losing any of them from the education process would be tragic and needless. Seeing Nicholas stumble reading words of completely gratuitous difficulty is painful. The reading assignments – although surely edited -- always contain words that cannot be comprehended or related in any deducible way to the child's spoken vocabulary. They simply have to be memorized.

Nicholas is going to do fine. He has a disciplined family, a large support system, and plenty of ability. Nicholas is not a problem and he can certainly prosper in the world as it is. He most definitely is not part of the *problem* which we hear so much about in today's schools. But why do we persist in making his task so needlessly difficult? It's the subject matter that's at fault. For the love of little children, let's change it.

IAN MORLEY DUCK, b. 1933 Kamloops, British Columbia, Canada; BSc 55 Queen's University, Kingston, Ontario, Canada; Research Assistant 55-56 University of British Columbia; PhD 61 California Institute of Technology; Research Associate 61-63 University of Southern California; from Research Associate to Professor of Physics and Astronomy 1963- present -- Rice University, Houston, Texas. Theoretical research in nuclear and particle physics from ev to Gev; radiative capture of light nuclei, muon capture, bremsstrahlung in proton-proton scattering, Fadeev equations, resonant pion production in nucleon-nucleon scattering, quark model of nucleon structure, models of color confinement, quark-gluon plasma excitation in antiproton annihilation in heavy nuclei, fine structure of the baryon octet-decuplet spectrum. Most recently co-author with E.C.G. Sudarshan of

(1) **Pauli and the Spin-Statistics Theorem**
    (World Scientific, 1997),

(2) **Toward an Understanding of the Spin-Statistics Theorem**, *Am. J. Phys.* 66(4), 284 (1998),and

(2) **100 Years of Planck's Quantum**
    (World Scientific, 2000).

**GOD HELP
ALL LITTLE CHILDREN
READ, WRITE and SPELL**

using

MODULAR ENGLISH

for

EASY UNIVERSAL LITERACY

by

Ian Duck

CHAPTER ONE: THE PROBLEM OF THE ENGLISH LANGUAGE.

Sec I.1: Introduction.

Two billion people worldwide use English daily, more than a billion of these as a first language. Ironically, only about three percent of these are in England. The vast majority -- about one billion -- owe their use of the language to their history as British colonial subjects in Eastern Asia and Africa. Access to the middle and upper classes in the colonial empire depended on a facility in the rulers' language which became and has remained not only a symbol but also a determinant of status.

The last fifty years of Pax Americana and the economic imbalance between west and east, north and south has greatly increased the worldwide dominance of the English language. This dominance shows every sign of increasing and conceivably of becoming total among the literate fraction of people. Already English completely dominates the international science vocabulary and its literature.

There certainly are locally competitive languages: Spanish, Japanese, Russian, Chinese, Arabic. However the only trans-territorial examples -- Spanish and Chinese -- are, by and large, not trans-ethnic; and are being constantly eroded by and permeated by English.

We raise the question -- is English well suited to the task of being the universal language? Our answer will be both a yes and a no.

On the one hand, a qualified 'yes' for oral communication in the sense that English has the most extensive vocabulary of all languages; and is not significantly worse than any other language in terms of its logical and grammatical structure, and is distinctly better than some. But on the other hand, the answer must be a resounding 'no' for written communication. Without regard to its relative merit (of which we are -- and intend to remain -- blissfully ignorant), the English language as written is in dire need of a thoroughgoing housecleaning to make it more accessible, less arcane and ambiguous, and quite simply *easier to learn*.

Sec I.2: Reforming English. Cons and Pros.

We really do not take great exception to the vocabulary, or even to the grammar.   Our immediate concern is the **_SPELLING_**! The point we will make and support at great length is that spelling needs to be simplified, clarified, made consistent and unambiguous and finally, and above all, made ultimately and completely **_PHONETIC_**.

We can hear the screams of outrage from all sides already. This suggestion has been made many times, always completely ineffectually. If it ever does become a serious consideration – which is our sole purpose here – it will no longer be viewed with benign bewilderment, but will be regarded as a mortal threat to the very fabric of our status quo. It will be vociferously rejected as a plague which will

> (1) destroy the language and with it
> (2) all literature, books, libraries,
> (3) history, culture,
> (4) educational standards and foundations,
> (5) laws, contracts, legal system, even civil order. On an even darker note, it will be accused of
> (6) fobbing off the lower classes with 'Ebonics'; of
> (7) debasing English into 'Gullah' -- a patois or dialect -- or rather into a myriad of these; of
> (8) degrading and irreversibly damaging the hard-earned gains of the undereducated; of
> (9) seeking to create a permanent caste system distinguished by the quality of their language; and on and on.

But the main reason for the outrage that will greet the suggestion of this radical revision of the written English language is that it would threaten the principal foundation of the elevated status occupied by the mandarins of our society -- the

4

educated elite -- which is their dominating facility from an early age with the written language. This facility has been enforced as the primary criterion for an ill-defined quality called 'intelligence', which in turn is our society's major measure of a person's worth as a human being. There obviously are others: beauty, talent, character,.....; but we are soon reduced to terms more suitable for describing our favorite pet like honesty, dependability, and so on. It is a short list and intelligence is at or near the top.

There are other measures of intelligence: pattern recognition, game playing, puzzle solving come to mind. They probably *do* have a positive correlation with the ability to quickly master spelling, reading, and arithmetic. These are obviously all birds of a feather and all test similar capacities. They are all probably equally damaging to the psyche of those who are tested and found lacking. How many of us who excelled at these exercises persevered at things -- music, art, sport, speech, foreign language, chess, bridge ..... come to mind in my own particular case -- where our early performances were miserably bad? How many of us who quickly mastered the rules and exceptions of spelling were defeated at a later (and much larger) stage -- self-esteem fully intact or at least carefully rationalized -- by the abstractions of mathematics and philosophy, by the myriad details of chemistry and biology, by a complete lack of resonance with poetry and art? We simply take comfort in our front row seats at the opera and are quite unthreatened by all the beauty of which we can be only a spectator. But we were not forced over and over again into unremitting confrontation and unrelenting failures attempting these difficult and even impossible tasks; certainly not at the earliest and most critically impressionable phase of our education; and certainly not with all the profound consequences -- visited on every young child who flounders -- of being weighed in the balance and found wanting.

People recall with smug amusement the many ways Einstein was deemed inadequate in his early education. All his life he thought slowly and seemingly painfully, and spoke in obscure tortured phrases. What would happen to this genius on an academic achievement test with 500 nonsense multiple choice questions to be answered at the rate of ten per minute? It's fully conceivable that he would have refused to participate. And even if he had participated it's quite probable his potential would not have been identified.

You might well respond that it is not the mission of elementary education to identify isolated genius, but to make functional the vast majority of ordinary children -- the fat center of some bell curve, IQ's between 90 to 110 or 80 to 120, whatever that might mean. I have no quarrel with that. I do quarrel with the testing itself which robs the education process of all freedom of choice, any joy of learning, and any self respect for anyone who once falls off the unicycle of the test process. Once a student falters then that student is under extreme duress ever after. If a student panics and is not able to produce under test conditions, then the stress is going to become ever greater; and panic, failure, rebellion, depression, apathy, and eventually psychosis can be expected as an ever accelerating downward spiral; until all hope is extinguished and the child is *permanently* damaged and rendered at the very least untestable and at the very worst unreachable and unteachable. Standardized testing is an abomination; but it is a separate issue and one not to be addressed here again.

What I wish to quarrel with here is the unremitting persistence of the education process in forcing All Little Children through the long, complicated, arbitrary, and basically senseless process -- completely lacking any intellectual substance -- of learning an antiquated written language which is infinitely jury-rigged and an on-going source of pain and frustration to almost half the world.

Sec I.3: Hidden Costs of the Status Quo.

If All Little Children emerged from this experience undamaged, there would be no serious problem. All those with IQ's above 100 would have succeeded in various degrees (or more likely, all those who succeeded would be judged to have IQ's above 100); the remaining half would go on to new subjects more suitable to their abilities. The cost would be purely economic -- perhaps one half the educational cost of the first six years, say $15,000 per student for six years of instruction in reading and spelling. For a first estimate, suppose that half the students (IQ's over 100) learn everything, half the students (IQ's under 100) learn nothing. Half the money has been spent fruitlessly. $7500 per student has been expended for no return. If we could make the subject more accessible then perhaps we could extend our 'learning curve' to include 80% of the students (with IQ's over ~90). In this case, 20% or only $3000 per student has been expended for no return. This of course is a most naive estimate, but it serves to demonstrate that our wealthy society can easily afford this aspect of the cost of teaching (and even failing to teach) the English language.

The real cost is elsewhere, and is traditionally associated with certain buzz-words that have been hoo-hawed into disrepute by educational reactionaries. These words include 'ego', 'self-esteem', 'psyche'. We prefer to characterize the damage done to students by the humiliation of repeated failure and repeated negative evaluations as a 'post-traumatic stress disorder'. It resides somewhere in most of us and creates a phobia which keeps us from ever again risking failure and humiliation, from repeating negative experiences, and -- at its worst -- from ever again *really, really* putting our whole heart and soul and full effort and undivided attention into *any* new enterprise where we might be judged *one more time* as a failure. This is the **_REAL COST_** of trying to teach All Little Children the infinite arcana of the written English language. The indications are that the damage is irreversible and progressive, manifesting itself in negative behavior directed at self (through degrading actions like substance abuse, body piercing, tattoos, sexual promiscuity) and others (through criminal behavior). The actual financial burden on society resulting from the inaccessibility of written English far transcends the trivial amount spent in elementary education. The trauma inflicted on elementary school children in their struggle to achieve literacy in English must be acknowledged as one of the major causes -- quite possibly *the* major cause -- of alienation and antisocial behavior in our society.

Trauma occurs in all degrees but even where not dramatic or catastrophic the results can be profound: A lifelong aversion to reading and writing, and to the risks of education. A lifelong insecurity in one's own thought processes leading to a sense of inferiority and a reluctance to compete, resulting in limited career goals. In young males, the results -- certainly compounded with other negative influences -- in extreme cases can lead to a long period of antisocial and eventually criminal behavior; of lashing out in a frustrated reaction against a society which has rejected them and which they have given up trying to please, and in which they have given up all hope of success.

Every family has felt the pain of a loved one who has been defeated by an inability to cope with the education experience. The results last a lifetime. We realize that abilities differ, not everyone can excel, not everyone is meant to be a scholar -- all the old rationalizations. And everyone has to achieve what comfort they can within their own limitations. Nonetheless, we will argue that the elementary education experience can be made astoundingly more accessible to 20 to 30% more people than at present. Obviously we can expect a corresponding reduction in the effort required by those now being reached. The change we propose not only will save time, money, and energy -- all of which can be put to good use by broadening and deepening the curriculum -- but also and most important, it will save children. The attitude and receptivity of All Little Children now struggling will be spared the trauma associated with attaining literacy in English by modernizing and rationalizing the traditional written English language into a fully phonetic Modular English form.

Sec I.4: A Better World After Language Reform.

To reiterate, our goal is *radical* reform of the spelling of the English language; to eradicate inconsistencies, ambiguities, obscurities, absurdities and obfuscations; all with the objective of achieving a new, modern, and Modular English written language which is completely user-friendly, less time consuming, expensive, frustrating and discouraging, especially in the education of elementary school students; thereby freeing time from repetitious drills on conventions and special cases which are intrinsically without intellectual content. The great economy of time, energy and expense achieved by making simpler the spelling, writing, and reading of the English language can then usefully be invested in subject matter containing ideas of both interest and consequence. Modular English will expedite the whole education process.

In this world of proliferating complexity and educational requirements; where the illiterate and under-educated will be marginalized and excluded at ever increasing peril to human survival; it is imperative that the very medium of communication be made most readily accessible to all people. Our suggested revision of the English language is the most direct step conceivable in this direction; it might well be the *only* such step since traditional written English, if left in place, would always block and frustrate any other reforms. Once reform is adopted, the transition could be complete in less than a decade and the future of universal human discourse set on a rational foundation. Traditional written English is a Berlin Wall imprisoning the world's illiterate -- our own children and grandchildren included -- in a regime of ignorance and poverty. When we tear down the wall, millions will pour across the artificial boundary that has kept them in servitude and they will then be free to participate in a world better for everyone.

Who could conceivably take such an action? And how? And when?

'How' is easy. 'Who' and 'when' involve gigantic political decisions and actions which will require at least as great an act of collective wisdom as humankind has ever displayed. The USA would probably have to do it alone by fiat. It is admittedly difficult to imagine. One possible scenario would have a nationwide general strike of all elementary school children, powered and directed over the internet, in which six to ten year old children organize to adamantly refuse to read anything but Modular English texts of every subject, which they would download on their computers free from Bill Gates, still angered after the break-up of Microsoft. Can you imagine? All Little Children dictating rationality to the whole disputatious, venal,

9

corrupt, self-serving, war-mongering, gun-toting, rapacious, murdering, thieving, fornicating, lying, cheating, drunken, stoned, lazy, self-centered, self-satisfied, reactionary, retrograde, conservative adult lot of us. What historic fun! So we have to convince Bill Gates to pay for it. And we will get Oprah to marshal all the mothers to the cause. It's as good as done!

And there is no other time like now. Every day we waste is more children we waste.

In the following chapters we explore in great detail the ramifications of this proposal to revise the spelling of the English language. These ramifications include:

(1) the impact on elementary education; examples of outrageously arbitrary and capricious spellings which defy understanding and deter and exhaust all students.

(2) a brief history of the English language; Webster's Americanized spelling as a welcome but weak and inadequate precursor; examples of other changes, none sufficient; excerpts from the classics.

(3) specific changes; a new but very familiar phonetic alphabet; easy examples; hard examples.

(4) excerpts from Pope, Shakespeare, Auden, etc; old and new, side by side.

(5) applications in fiction, newspapers, philosophy, and science.

(6) We are then better able to appreciate the problems of non-uniqueness characteristic of phonetic spelling.

(7) We next discuss the sociology of language reform in terms of sources of opposition and support; and its impact on various social groups.

(8) We explore the importance of successful language reform on the increased education requirements necessary in the modern world.

(9) We expand on our thesis that the difficulties of traditional written English in elementary education are responsible for widespread Post-Traumatic Stress Disorder which underlies much ongoing sociological pathology.

(10) Finally, we outline an implementation campaign to make Modular English reform a universal reality in the US by 2005.

Sec I.5: Concluding Remarks.

A crucial element in the development of Modular English reform has been the experience of actually using the new written language in realistic situations to express complex thoughts in sophisticated vocabularies. What becomes immediately clear -- and probably should have been anticipated from the start -- is that the spoken language *cannot* be written phonetically in a *unique* way, in fact quite the contrary. Does this mean we should just stack our arms in abject defeat? Or fold our tents and slink silently from the field? We believe not. The stakes in this battle are too great to give up: we are seeking to benefit All Little Children for all time. We must not -- we cannot -- fail.

Our conclusion is that written language reform must include something more fundamental than just a new array of rules and conventions for spelling. It requires not *just* these technical changes to make the written English Language accessible. Successful language reform also requires a change of pedagogic philosophy. The new philosophy must abandon the old absolutist attitude that there is one *right* way and every other is *wrong* and therefore worthless and to be condemned. This strict old-fashioned attitude is no longer enforced anywhere else except in elementary education and in some areas of mathematics. The new philosophy must accept that the written language -- like the spoken language -- should permit some latitude, some judgement, in writing and spelling. There should be a continuum between good spelling which is easy to read and -- let us not say bad or even unacceptable but instead -- let's say difficult spelling which is hard or impossible to read. Spelling becomes a matter of judgement, and also an individual matter depending on accent, elision, and emphasis.

CHAPTER TWO: THE PHONICS WARS.

Sec II.1: The Arguments For and Against Phonics.

The education establishment has convinced itself -- and large numbers of like-minded people -- that phonics is some form of cheating, that it is ethically and morally somehow wrong to attack a problem with all of our God-given senses. These same people have no qualms about training-wheels on bicycles or T-ball for beginning little leaguers, but they find it corrupting to make reading and spelling easier by using both senses of *sound* as well as *sight*.

There is always a mixed agenda lurking somewhere in the background while All Little Children are struggling to master the intricacies of English. Favorites are character development, discipline, developing powers of memory, concentration and diligence, and -- unwittingly God preserve us -- of identifying and rewarding merit and even of inflicting suffering where there need be none. A sadistic puritanical impulse seems to compel us to bend helpless creatures (All Little Children) to our will -- always for their own good, of course -- as we were bent. The justification for this could only be the wonderful effect it had on us! Let's examine this premise.

First of all, the argument is made only by the survivors; and even then only by a marginal group which has never really got over the experience and is still wearing their modest success as a medal of honor to distinguish themselves from those who didn't survive. Neither group -- the failures who are now mute because of shame and apathy, or the marginal survivors who have risen from victim to trusty to guard and zealous advocate of the status quo -- was greatly benefited by the experience.

Secondly, the notion that mind like muscle benefits from every senseless repetitious exercise is probably wrong on both counts. Exercise, yes. But exercise even of muscles has to be carefully planned not to damage tendons, dull reflexes, restrict agility, and ultimately to rob us of pleasure and enthusiasm for the very goals toward which we are striving to improve ourselves. Surely the mind is at least as subtle as the body.

The single greatest motivation to successful participation in every educational enterprise is a feeling of accomplishment, which must be carefully nurtured and never, NEVER exposed as an artifact of the teacher. No dirty tricks! No humiliations. No failures.

Yet reading, writing and spelling are full of such negative experiences because there is no continuous progression or practice which can prepare a child to read or spell words which have no apparent association with our spoken language. And here is where the puritans exult. Memorize it for the good of your soul, you sinner. Remember it for the sake of your salvation, or be damned. And enjoy your pain. And since the language is largely irrational, there is really no alternative. We have suffered with this situation for at least the last 500 years. It has done incalculable damage to generation upon generation, and it's time to set it right.

The puritans among us argue first of all that memory training is essential to learning. This has an element of truth, but it reflects a mean form of learning devoid of critical thought and understanding. All learning worth dignifying by inclusion in the education process requires the ability to remember and to recall ideas and even facts, but these are not stored helter-skelter in some bottomless pit of the mind, nor even arranged neatly in some mental file cabinet. They are more analogous to the pathways by which the squirrel of our consciousness scurries about in the tenuous branches of the forest of our mind. The connections are everything, and they are only ordered by understanding. So anything but the meanest sort of information cannot usefully be memorized as a factoid -- an isolated and otherwise inconsequential fact -- as All Little Children are required to memorize arcane words. And even if memory development is the ultimate goal, why not practice the memorizing skill directly on the things to be memorized rather than making a gratuitous detour for a substantial portion of a child's life to memorize an arbitrary language. The greatest stimulus to memory is *interest* which different people find in different places, but rarely if ever in such meaningless distinctions as between '-ible' and '-able', or '-full' and '-ful', and so on *ad nauseum*.

An argument commonly used against phonetics is that it is too slow. One should not try to sound out words piecemeal, we are told, but should learn to recognize them at a glance. Well, of course it is slow to try to deduce a word from its parts when there is no logical connection. But if there *were* a logical connection, as there will be in the modular phonetic language we are proposing, then the rational approach to learning by analysis and synthesis of the component parts *would* work. Both senses-- sight and sound -- would reinforce each other, rather than interfere with and contradict each other. The senses would experience a positive cognitive resonance rather than a negative cognitive dissonance as is now so frequently the case. Just these effects are actually observed in recent experiments measuring brain activity during speed-reading: tumultuous brain activity in people reading very non-phonic English; relatively tranquil brain activity in people reading Italian, a much more uniquely phonic language.

Sec II.2: Traditional English Spelling – Demoralizing? YES!

Each cognitive dissonance is a destructive experience which erodes a child's confidence in sight and sound, until soon the child abandons all hope in the face of a game so arbitrary and, quite literally, senseless (*i.e.*, without sense as in outside the senses). All Little Children find themselves in a no-win situation where they can only trust their senses in situations they already know, which is to say that they cannot trust their senses at all. No wonder they sink into an apathetic -- or even hostile and aggressive -- state where they refuse to attempt any kind of pro-active solution to the dilemma (*i.e.*, embarrassing and perplexing situation). The only way for them to succeed is to memorize each word individually, and they can't do that either because there's always a new one waiting to trip them up. The reaction is like that of a wild animal trapped in a maze. The first reaction is a frenzy of hyper-activity, but it soon lapses into apathy. Is it any wonder that a little child sentenced to such a life without hope of success or release would withdraw into an irreversible near-catatonic state? The only recourse is a defense mechanism of psychological withdrawal and a refusal to participate in further infliction of his own suffering by dropping out -- in mind and spirit if not in body.

There can be no greater motivation to change the written language than this devastating impact on elementary education. To maintain and encourage the positive attitude that *every* child brings to school on that first day, ___**SUCCESS**___ is the key. Failure -- complete, permanent, and obvious to all including the victim -- is the soul-destroying experience of some 30% of All Little Children when confronted with the arbitrary, capricious, inconstant, infinitely variable and fickle so-called 'rules' of English spelling. Every rule is made to be broken. Every rule is defined by its exception. Can you imagine an arithmetic in which 8 times 7=56 except when it is preceded by a prime not including 3 and 5, when it is 53, unless the ......? Of course not. That would be nonsense and no one would tolerate it.

The rules of English spelling are not one whit more interesting or fruitful, or blessed with more intellectual content and consequence, than the poor stupid example I managed to scribble down above. They, in fact, are not *blessed* by their consequences, but *damned* by them. For consequences there are, and it is -- dare I use the sacred word -- an ongoing holocaust of destruction wrought upon helpless children.

To assure success in primary education, consistency and integrity of the rules of the game are crucial. Inconsistency and fickleness not only undermine and permanently damage the child's self-confidence, but they plant the seed of alienation and hostility in the child's mind that the world is a hostile and punitive place where he has no chance of success within rules he can neither comprehend -- because they are incomprehensible -- nor apply -- because having once, twice, ... failed, he goes through various stages of loathing, fear, panic, apathy, withdrawal, hostility, revenge, ...

Sec II.3: The Sociological Impact.

In effect, the outrageous demands of the written English language are serving the purpose of the old-fashioned British 11+ exams, which was to separate the sheep from the goats, the men from the boys, the educatable professional upper middle class who would go on to higher education and all its perks of ease, comfort, respect, affluence, and power; from the uneducatable lower class who would not.

We take pride that ours is a much more egalitarian society and in some respects it is. We do not give up easily on anyone. A tremendous amount time, effort, and money is lavished on All Little Children trying to give them the best our wealthy society can offer. Bless our hearts! But then we turn right around and negate all this effort. We are not brutish or stupid enough to force upon them a false arithmetic based on specious assumptions with some sly intention that by mastering it they will somehow be the better for it. No, but we do the moral equivalent to persist in abusing them with the senseless conventions of an arcane and archaic written language which has been criticized from the beginning by the likes of Samuel Johnson, Benjamin Franklin, Noah Webster, and many others of manifest intellect, ability, and judgement.

Returning to the question of phonetic reading being slower than sight reading, why would anyone argue anything else? The point is -- with a rationalized modular phonetic language -- phonics is the way to *start* reading and to *continuously* and *continually* improve and -- hopefully, eventually – merge smoothly into sight recognition at full speed. The merit is in the words *continuously*, *continually*, and *smoothly*. If sight recognition ever fails, the phonics safety-net is always there. There are no dirty tricks, no humiliations, no failures, no trauma.

Does this mean that everyone can learn to read anything? Of course not. Words, content, ideas, and concepts are going to be as complicated, intricate, subtle, and demanding as ever. In fact there need be no change or reduction of vocabulary, and no compromise or dilution of the grammatical sophistication of the language. If a word is not in your spoken vocabulary, it is not going to be in your reading vocabulary. On the other hand, once you see a written word you will be able to pronounce it. Exactly? Correctly? Perhaps not *exactly*, but modulo certain accents, yes.

Jonathan Swift, the British satirist and polemicist (1667--1745), wrote against phonetics at a time when spellings were proliferating and had not yet stabilized to any standard usage, which was first done in Samuel Johnson's (1709--1784) dictionary (conceived in 1746, published in 1755). Swift's problem with phonetics arose from the radical diversity of dialects on the most regional of scales in Britain. Swift's remarks are amusing but we will argue no longer relevant:

> Another cause which hath contributed not a little to the maiming of our Language, is a foolish Opinion, advanced of late Years, that we ought to spell exactly as we speak; which beside the obvious Inconvenience of utterly destroying our Etymology, would be a thing we should never see an End of. Not only the several Towns and Counties of *England* have different ways of Pronouncing, but even here in *London*, they clip their Words after one Manner about the Court, another in the City, and a third in the Suburbs ...... All which reduced to Writing would entirely confound Orthography. Yet many People are so fond of this Conceit, that it is sometimes a difficult matter to read modern Books and Pamphlets; where the Words are so curtailed, and varied from their original Spelling, that whoever hath been used to plain *English*, will hardly know them by sight.

Swift misses the court on every volley. No one is suggesting that *we* write as *we* speak, with free license. There will be a dictionary, and we might even look words up to check their spelling, as now. The difference is obvious: a one-to-one and reversible relation between speaking and spelling. Not necessarily in accord with every dialect, but in accord with some great central norm -- termed by some a mid-Atlantic accent. The mass-media has more or less established such a norm, and regional dialects are being further eroded by population migrations and mixing. So this fear no longer has any foundation, and was probably gratuitous in the first instance anyway.

Further, when Swift refers to the '*inconvenience* of utterly destroying *our* Etymology', we have to wonder: Whose inconvenience? Whose etymology? He is obviously referring to a minuscule educated elite. Why would a six year old be inconvenienced by easier spelling? Why would any illiterate person, or anyone who had been disenfranchised by the inability to spell, feel possessive -- or anything positive -- about *our* etymology? No, this is the convenience and the etymology of a very small, very self-satisfied Brahmin caste of word-smiths. The devil take them.

The last lines say it all: 'would entirely confound Orthography (*i.e.,* the art of spelling) ..... whoever hath been used to plain English, will hardly know them by sight.' But surely, the Swifts among us are blessed with the mental dexterity to quickly master the new rationalized phonetic Modular English language. How can they in conscience condemn a much larger number of people to struggle endlessly and fruitlessly with the present form of the language? I hate to suggest that the answer is self-aggrandizement.

Sec II.4: Defend WHAT Status Quo?   There IS NO Status Quo!

Johnson, in contrast to Swift, had a very tolerant attitude about the language which he viewed as a living thing possessed and created and changed by the people who use it, not something to be controlled by an elite or Academy. In the preface to his dictionary, he emphasized the impossibility to:

> ..... fix our language, ... put a stop to those alterations which time and chance have hitherto been suffered to make in it without opposition. ..... may the lexicographer be derided ..... [who] imagine[s] that his dictionary can embalm a language ..... sounds are too volatile and subtile for legal restraints ....

These remarks were presumably about changes of vocabulary and pronunciation, but not of radical changes in spelling. Even so, Johnson's is a liberal, permissive and extremely pragmatic voice which we will take as encouragement to construct the new English.

Reactionary defenders of the status quo of the English language seem to be in a state of denial, unable to accept that the language is shifting constantly under their dragging feet. They have the typical lower-middle class boot-licking attitude that anything is all right provided it happens slowly enough, is ordained by some authority figure, and does not threaten their petty hegemony.

Early authority figures -- most notably including Thomas Jefferson, Benjamin Franklin, John Adams, and Noah Webster -- each with impeccable intellectual *and* revolutionary credentials, have lent respectability to language reform. Unfortunately, the reforms -- consciously moderated from the beginning by a too timorous Webster, perhaps exhausted by a labor commensurate with Johnson's -- were too conservative to have any *real* impact on the difficulty of the language. After almost 200 years the few and ineffectual changes have become fossilized into the standard spelling of an American English which is only a small improvement over the British original. A typical example of the changes formalized in Webster's 1828 dictionary is the dropping of the 'u' in the British spelling of colour, labour, neighbour, *etc*. As welcome as this simplification is, it clearly does not eliminate the dichotomy between 'labor' and 'neighbor' which has its origin in the remote past, in the obscure and – for *all* elementary school children and 99&44/100% of the rest of us -- the ***completely*** irrelevant origins of these words. Better we should bury the etymological details than another generation of elementary school students. Simplify! Rationalize!! Phoneticize!!! Some unemployable word-smith can keep track of the distinction between the Latin *labor* the verb to work, and the old-English *neah gebur* for someone living nearby. These useless appendages encoded into the language threaten to drown us all.

Benjamin Franklin -- the self-educated printer of inestimably high intellect -- was the progenitor of Webster's dictionary, through his 1768 paper *A Scheme for a New Alphabet and a Reformed Mode of Spelling*. We will return in a separate chapter to the details of Franklin's failed suggestion, which in fact we intend to clone from its mammoth DNA. In the meantime, we recommend it for a brief history of the revolutionary turmoil of the birth of American English, and especially for the prescience of Adams on the future world dominance of America and of English which we are witnessing after 200 years. It is ironical that the dominance is finally coming about for technological reasons that not even Franklin could have imagined, even though he was so eminently involved in its scientific origin. Our primary interest here is to wrap our radical and revolutionary intentions in the impregnable cloak of the respectability of these immortal Founding Fathers who unfortunately fell short of their similar goals.

In summary, we declare the Phonics Wars to be over; and the objections to phonics to be made obsolete and irrelevant by a formulation of the spelling of English akin to but greatly improved over that proposed by Franklin 232 years ago. The new language will be designed specifically and purposefully with the learning needs of elementary school children foremost in mind. But everyone -- whether or not they struggled in this phase of their education -- will have easy access to the new spelling. The new formulation of the spelling of English will have as its primary goals the following obviously desirable features:

- (i) it will be phonetic,
- (ii) modular,
- (iii) unambiguous,
- (iv) easy to read and spell,
- (v) and it will be readily accessible to an estimated 30% more of the population than currently.

Sec II.5: A Word of Warning.

There is no question that what we are proposing will be revolutionary. There will be vociferous opposition and there will be considerable expense. But I maintain that there need be NO casualties and NO losers. On the contrary, the current horrendous casualty rate lost to *de facto* functional illiteracy will be reduced from a guesstimated 30% to 10% as we extend the accessibility of English to many of those now excluded. Furthermore, the tremendous benefits of *including* many more people in the education process will extend to everyone including those now prospering. Those students now fully capable of the demands of English will be able to achieve the same mastery with much less time and effort, freeing them to pursue other academic interests. Older people who have passed successfully through this phase of education will -- like Swift -- have no difficulty accommodating the changes. They can find many motivations to do so for the sake of their own children and grandchildren. No family is without a loved one who has been made to suffer needlessly and destructively by the present form of English. The psychological and sociological damage to school children now marginalized, traumatized, and ultimately rejected by the education system will be reduced by a guesstimated factor of three. The direct monetary cost of reading, writing, and spelling education will be reduced tremendously, and the money, time, and effort saved can be redirected with great benefit to other areas.

A word of warning: Like any revolution, there can be NO half measures. There can not be a 'fast track' of the language as we now know it and a 'slow track' of the new phonetic language. There will be a lot of people who will want to split off as an elite caste studying the old language. It ***must not happen***, and we address this problem also.

Clearly, the imposition of such a change will take tremendous resolve for any society. Probably only the US has the spirit and flexibility, the drive and adventurousness, the *joie de vivre*, the unbounded freedom from a tradition bound past, ... to even embark on such an adventure, but moreover to make it succeed overnight. The experience will be like a currency change. One morning we will just do it. The New York Times will look startlingly different one morning, and within a week we will have all made the successful transition. It will generate a tremendous bond in the society, that we have spontaneously had a vast intellectual spring cleaning which has at last cleaned the cupboards and closets and attics of our minds of all the old trash. What will we do with all the garbage?

The rest of the world will follow in amazement, but they will follow and benefit and be grateful as will all humankind forever. Let's just do it.

CHAPTER THREE:
BENJAMIN FRANKLIN'S PHONICS.

Sec III.1: A Brief Introduction.

Benjamin Franklin while a printer in Philadelphia made a foray into radical language reform with his 1768 proposal

" A Scheme for a New Alphabet and a Reformed Mode of Spelling",

which he finally published in 1779. Whether he was serious or this was purely 'tongue-in-cheek' and simply intended to fill the pages of his Poor Richard's Almanac is not clear. In any case, his proposal was never accepted outside his own small group of personal friends who sometimes practiced it to humor him. There is still much to learn from this particular Franklin experiment, but something much more important we should learn -- never too late, I hope -- from Franklin himself, and that is the art of advocacy. He advised diffidence, modesty, gentle words, and understatement to advance even the most passionately held of causes. It is important, he counsels, to let prospective supporters discover the merits of an idea for themselves, and even to feel that they have a part in discovering the idea itself.

In spite of its failure and many manifest faults, and in spite of the fact that it has been buried under an ongoing tide of failed language reforms, Franklin's scheme is worth studying for its cultural and historical interest, as well as for its amusement. In fact, we won't study any other -- if they are not obvious and easy we have no use for them. If they are obvious and easy we have no need for them. So the devil take all 200 years of the pusillanimous lot of them. Our purpose is not scholarship, but action. Ours is not primarily a tactical plan but rather a call to arms for a strategic campaign. We *will* propose a quite specific '*scheme*' to reform the language, but we have in mind a different purpose and a different set of principles than those of past reformers which have proven to be totally ineffectual. But first let's see what Franklin did.

The word 'foray' -- a raid for plunder, forage, ultimately *sustenance* -- is appropriate for Franklin's insatiable need to sustain Poor Richard. The warlike metaphor hardly begins to describe the disputatious character of the reactionary response from those who defend the faith of the received traditional written English language against any and all intrusions of phonics, let alone the radical changes which Franklin advocated and the different but still radical changes we suggest.

Some of Franklin's suggestions did find their way into Webster's reforms [ref Abraham Tauber, *Word Study* V31-3, 4-6 (1956)]: for example, the American 'jail' replaces the British 'gaol', 'humor' replaces 'humour', 'plow' replaces 'plough', etc; and many more have become the American standard.

Tauber goes further to credit Franklin with recognizing and analyzing the basic principles of phonetics, if not actually inventing the subject. Franklin concluded that six of our 26 letters are redundant (c, j, q, w, x, y); and actually designed the print for substitute symbols representing: the '*a*' as in 'b*a*ll', the *th* as in '*th*ink', the '*th*' as in '*th*y', the '*sh*' as in '*sh*ip', the '*ng*' as in 'repeati*ng*', and the '*u*' in '*u*nto'. Few of his ideas we find to be useful, and our proposal will not be as radical or as doctrinaire as Franklin's. Our projected language reforms do not aspire to be perfectly phonetic. Nor do we ever require any special symbol for common sounds like 'sh' or 'ng'; nor do we make such subtle distinctions like the different emphases as above on the 'th's'.

Franklin made distinctions in sounds based on the different anatomical actions required in their production. We won't do that either. We *will* follow Franklin in having no silent vowels, and a (nearly) unique sound associated with each vowel and each consonant. We must keep constantly in mind the purpose of *our* language reform: it is to help *All Little Children* learn *without trauma* to read, write, and spell. It is **_NOT_** to design a phonetic system complex enough to take care of every exigency.

Tauber quotes a letter Franklin wrote defending his proposal against objections raised by his friend Polly Stevenson. Franklin responded:

"The objection you make to rectifying our alphabet, that it will be attended by inconveniences and difficulties, is a natural one; for it always occurs when any reformation is proposed, whether in religion, government, laws, and even down as low as roads and wheel carriages. The true question then is not whether there will be no difficulties or inconveniences but whether the conveniences will not, on the whole, be greater than the inconveniences. In this case, the difficulties are only in the beginning of the practice; when they are once overcome the advantages are lasting. To either you or me, who spell well in the present mode, I imagine the difficulty of changing that mode for the new is not so great but that we might perfectly get over it in a week's writing. As to those who do not spell well, if the two difficulties Are compared, viz., that of teaching them the true spelling in the present mode and that of teaching them the new alphabet and the new spelling according to it, I am confident that the latter would be by far the least. They naturally fall into the new method already, as much as the imperfection of the alphabet will admit of; their present bad spelling is only bad because contrary to the present bad rules; under the knew rules it would be good. The difficulty of learning to spell well in the old way is so great that few attain it, thousands and thousands writing on to old age without ever being able to acquire it. 'Tis, besides, a difficulty continually increasing, as the sound varies more and more from the spelling; and to foreigners it makes the learning to pronounce our language as written in our books, almost impossible."

It is a tribute to Franklin's genius brought to bear on an obvious problem that his concerns -- which were so on the mark -- still remain so important. What Franklin missed here in his first assessment was the *ever increasing magnitude* of the problem due to the overwhelming degree of class distinction made in our modern society based on the ability to read, write and spell; and ultimately to be educated and successful in the technological-corporate-professional world. Nor -- at least so far in our cursory reading -- did Franklin seem to recognize the brutal and lasting ego-damage done to little children by that first and *final* failure to demonstrate this fundamental capacity which has become our over-riding primary criterion of educability. The *finality* of the failure is almost guaranteed as a self-fulfilling prophecy for a delicate child at the age of 6 -- 10. That first failure and rejection -- even then, even to such a young child, so obviously an official adult judgement of their intrinsic worth in the view of the world -- is devastating. The trauma continues unabated because there is no escape from the ongoing reminders of their inadequacy and humiliations from their failures as long as they stay in school. In this respect, Franklin's was a kinder and gentler world than our own. In Franklin's world people had many ways to express their worth without first succeeding in becoming formally educated. We no longer have a frontier where self-taught rail-splitters can become lawyers, much less presidents of immortal memory. In our world, if you can't demonstrate the ability to read, write and spell by the age of 7, 8, 9, or 10 , you are damaged goods ***and you know it.***

Apparently Franklin's sister Mrs. Jane Mecom had trouble spelling. Franklin wrote her:

> ''You need not be concerned, in writing to me, about your bad spelling; for, in my opinion, as our alphabet now stands, the bad spelling or what is called so, is generally the best, as conforming to the sound of the letters and of the words. To give you an instance ....." (There followed an interminable shaggy-dog story, the point of which was the obvious merit of Franklin's new improved way of spelling 'wife' as 'yf', which was correctly interpreted only by a semi-literate servant.)

Our reformed language will not seek as great economies as did Franklin's and as do most others. Our aim will be not to trivially titillate some faux-intelligentsia, but rather to *change the direction of the whole world!!* We will give easy access to literacy and all its rewards -- the most important of which are the confidence, the time, the energy, and the opportunity to advance unobstructed to an education based on *ideas* and understanding, not -- as is now so much the case -- on memorization, rote learning, and arbitrary rules and their arbitrary exceptions.

No one can fail to recognize the massive increase in the amount of knowledge required of today's children compared -- in my own case – to 50-60 years ago. The burden on the education system is made even greater by many other influences: the distractions of the all pervading entertainment industry; the failure to maintain the status and salary of teachers; the disruption of families in modern city life; the economic, educational, and cultural diversity of the children; and the critical necessity to educate *everyone* for a viable economic place in a changing world. It is critically important that we do everything possible to remove all artificial barriers to learning. It is especially important to remove the artificial barriers to *learning the very medium of learning*: the written English Language.

No two people will ever agree on a 'best way' to reform the English language. Many people have quibbled and quarreled -- quite literally for *centuries* -- with practically no progress. All the 'practical people' and the 'political realists' agree that any effort is useless and not worth considering. Do they have any 'realistic' idea of the very 'practical' cost of teaching the reading, writing and spelling of our well-nigh impossible written English language to the 6 million new students who enter our American schools *every year*? Do they ever wonder what happens to the 1.5 million who fail to perform in reality, if not officially to be passed on to the next grade? What is the cost to our society of these children? What is the cumulative cost of people rejected at the very first hurdle of elementary education? It seems that the problem is vastly greater than even Franklin ever realized.

The magnitude worldwide is staggering -- the number of children in the English speaking part of the world must be greater by a factor of 10 to 20, the fraction of failures must be even greater than ours, primarily for the reason of poverty. It is no exaggeration to conjecture 100 million people a year seeking access to written English, and -- predicated on that -- meaningful access to much of the modern world. At least 30 million will be frustrated in their attempts to gain English literacy. What happens to these people? They are largely destined to be poor, diseased, hopeless, resentful, and to grow to hate us. And they outnumber us by an ever increasing factor currently about five to one. Think of the world wide magnitude of the wasted effort, the frustration, the failure -- all due to the arcane spelling of the English language.

Franklin expressed a concern for those already fully literate but having to change old habits. He concluded, and we agree, that this is surely a small adjustment compared to the advantages for people -- most importantly, All Little Children -- learning for the first time. For these and all future generations, there are *__NO__* disadvantages or inconveniences. All such straw-men erected by critics will be systematically demolished as we confront them, one-by-one, using the most elementary but compelling logic.

Franklin also dismissed the objection of etymologists that a change of spelling would obscure the word origins and thereby their meaning. Franklin stated the obvious: ''.... we don't look to etymology for the present meaning... It is from present usage only that the meaning of words is to be determined.''

As for the objection that a spelling reform would render present books useless, Franklin wrote -- and we fully concur: ''..whatever the difficulties and inconveniences now are, they will be more easily surmounted now than hereafter; and sometime or other it must be done, or our writing will become the same with Chinese as to the difficulty of learning and using it. And it would already have been such if we had continued the Saxon spelling and writing used by our forefathers.''

Franklin might well have added a fact that is little known, well guarded by empire-building librarians and their ilk, and only acknowledged with anguished reluctance by bibliophiles and authors. The fact is that the useful life of most books is *ZERO*. When we have removed these from the calculation, the useful life of books *which actually had a life to begin with, and were not still-born* still averages less than 5 years. A recent academic library survey [Duck, unpublished result] across broad subject lines showed that among those library books *which had ever circulated* (and were thus not relegated to secondary storage), 93% of the usage came in the first 5 years of their acquisition. The average number of checkouts after 5 years was 0.83. The conclusion is that the usage of old books is rare and largely limited to academic research purposes. Why should this be a consideration comparable to the education of All Little Children? The same hyper-literate elite will still be able to decipher the same books, the only difference being that it will be like reading Chaucer in the original archaic English.

Unfortunately, in spite of all his intellect and wit, and of a lifetime spent perfecting the arts of persuasion and politics, Franklin's writings on this subject were tedious and ineffectual. Furthermore, the details of his proposal were a confusion of obscure motives made worse by his introduction of new letters in the alphabet in place of various common sounds. A brief sampling of his method is sufficient to deter its further exploration:

"It is endeavoured to give the Alphabet a more natural Order; beginning firſt with the ſimple Sounds formed by the Breath, with none or very little help of Tongue, Teeth, and Lips, and produced chiefly in the windpipe. "Then coming forward to thoſe, formed by the Roof of the Tongue next to the Windpipe...."And laſtly, ending with the ſhutting up of the Mouth, or cloſing the Lips, while any Vowel is ſounding."

The 'ſ's of course were a standard printing flourish of the day, and not part of the reform.

Oswald [J.C. Oswald, *Benjamin Franklin Printer* (Doubleday, Page & Company, 1926), p.194] reproduces two verses in Franklin's reformed alphabet and spelling. We can only simulate his new letters with visually similar symbols, but the approximate result is shown next.

It is interesting and amusing to compare Franklin's phonics – line by line – to the Standard English (the second line in curly brackets {..}); and our Modular English (the third line in square brackets [..]). For the example in Modular English we will have to anticipate the developments of the next few chapters. Modular English is almost magically self-evident and we have no doubt that the reader will understand it on first sight, which is of course its purpose. It will not be strictly phonetic, but instead will strive for a *consistent modularity,* so that words are made up of basic modules.

Example of Franklin's Phonics:

So huen sɒm endjiel bɒi divɒin kɸmmand,
{So when some angel by divine command [1]-- SE}
[Soe wen sum aenjl bie divien komand -- ME]

Uiθ rɒizi☐ tempests seeks e gilti land,
{With rising tempests seeks a guilty land [2]}
[With riezing tempists seeks a giltee land]

(Sutχ az ɸv leet or peel Britania past,)
{(Such as of late o'er pale Britannia passed,) [3]}
[(Suc az uv laet or pael Britanya past,)]

Kalm and siriin hi drɒivs θi fiurips blast;
{Calm and serene he drives the furious blast [4]}
[Kom and sireen hee drievz thuh fyureeus blast]

And, pliiz'd θi ɸlmɒitis ɸrdɒrs tu p☐rfɸrm,
{And pleased the Almighty's orders to perform [5]}
[And pleezd thuh Olmieteez ordirz tuh pirform]

Rɒids in θi huɒrluind and dɒirekts θI stɸrm.
{Rides in the whirlwind and directs the storm. [6]}
[Riedz in thuh wirlwind and direkts thuh storm.]

So θi piur limpid striim, huen fɸul uiθ steens
{So the pure limpid stream when foul with stains [7]}

[Soe thuh puer limpid streem wen fowl with staenz]
φf ρξiη tφrents and disendiη reens,
{Of rising torrents or descending rains [8]}
[Uv riezing torents or disending raenz]

Uρrks itself kliir; and az it rρns rifρins;
{Works itself clear and as it runs refines; [9]}
[Wirks itself kleer and az it runz reefienz;]

Til bρi digriis, θi flotiη mirρr χρins,
{Till by degrees, thy floating mirror shines, [10]}
[Til bie digreez, thie floeting meerir shienz,]

Riflekts iitξ flφur θat φn its bφrdρr groz,
{Reflects each flower that on its border grows, [11]}
[Riflekts eec flowr that on its bordir groez,]

And e nu hev'n in its feer bρzρm χoz.
{And a new heaven in its fair bosom shows. [12]}
[And a nue hevn in its fer buhzum shoez.]

Sec III.2: Lessons Learned from Franklin.

At the level of quarrelsome quibbling, Franklin's phonics do not seem to achieve the very consistency which is its only *raison d'etre*. In the poem illustrating his scheme, there are persistent inconsistencies when rendering the final 's' as 's' when soft and sibilant; as 'z' when hard. In addition there is presumably a typographical error responsible for the different renderings of 'rising' which sensibly use 'iz' in line (2) but inexplicably to us uses 'ξ' in line (8). These might conceivably be the result of Oswald's carelessness and not Franklin's intent. However the poem does employ the rare type-font peculiar only to Franklin's printing press. Even though it was not specifically attributed to him, Oswald has many reproductions of Franklin's printing in this book copyrighted in 1917, and published in 1926. A primitive but quite effective means of photocopying existed even then so these probably *are* faithful copies of the original prints and our quarrel probably *is* with Franklin and not Oswald.

Problems arise with the sounds rendered as 's' in lines 7,8,9,10 (stains, rains, refines, shines) which are indistinguishable in our way of speaking from those rendered as 'z' in lines 11,12 (grows, shows). This would seem to be just the 'distinction without a difference' that phonics is intended to eliminate. Of course it's easy to correct: give them all a 'z', and also drives [line 4], orders [5], Almighty's [5], rides [6], runs [9], and degrees [10]; but (correctly) retain 's' for seeks [2], directs [6], torrents [8], works [9], reflects [11], and its [11,12]. As is correctly 'az'.

These trivial inconsistencies are troubling but easily corrected. The *real* problem with Franklin's scheme is that it raised such hob with the *simple* words which were and are ___**NOT**___ the problem. We find his enthusiasm for change-for-its-own-sake to be excessive, bordering on a self-defeating zealotry. This reaction is not unusual among proponents of lost causes, which is how we have come to view doctrinaire phoneticists. All their efforts seem sooner rather than later to disappear in a spiral of almost facetious cleverness which we hope to avoid.

Franklin's opening premises seem to have been the seed of many of his miss-steps and in fact are still a problem for strict phonetics. We list a few of his principles whose applications seem unconstructive:

(1) He abandons six familiar letters (c, j, q, w, x, y) because he finds them redundant. We will put them all (except q) to good and consistent use, and -- yes -- sometimes even to traditional use. The key element of our plan will be consistent use, although it will not necessarily be strictly phonetic. A too doctrinaire application of phonetics would require the use or sound of the letter to coincide closely if not exactly with the sound of its name. What possible use could anyone then find for 'double-you'? Obviously none. But change its name to something like 'whu' and then uses are everywhere. We don't require the name change, but instead suggest that

every letter have a **name** *and* a **job**. So 's' has the soft sibilant sound 'ess', but not the 'eh' part of its name, as in 's'ometime; but never the hard 'z' sound as in 'az'. The temptation to compress 'compress' too much to 'comprs' never arises and the rationalization 'compres' (although incomplete because we haven't yet dealt with the 'c' and the 'o' sounds) is readily and uniquely made; similarly for 'f, t, b, r, ...'. Their *names* are uniquely and suggestively but not *directly* connected to their *jobs* of sound usage.

(2) The connection between the name of a letter and the sound-job assigned to it will usually be traditional, but not always direct and therefore not really phonic. All we will require is uniqueness and consistency, and even here there will be minor compromises especially on emphasis. An example is Franklin's distinction between the 'th' sounds in 'thy' and 'thigh', which we will not make. It will suffice for the written language to suggest the spoken word, but the spoken word must easily and uniquely *dictate* the written word. How then do we distinguish homonyms? The answer is trivial: just as we do when speaking, by the context; and the onus is on the speaker to be unambiguous. In fact, a random sample of the pages of the dictionary [Oxford American Dictionary] shows that fewer than 1/10% of English words have homonyms, indicating that this is not a major consideration. So one spelling will have to suffice for both 'thy' and 'thigh', and -- anticipating our eventual language reform -- we use 'thie'.

(3) Franklin and many of his successors attempted to express frequently occurring sounds with a single symbol. Thus the sound '-ng' in the example is denoted by 'η' (not Franklin's original new font, but the Greek 'eta' used here for typographical convenience). Other examples are 'th-' (here theta θ), 'sh-' (here chi χ), and others. Our attitude on this is less doctrinaire and more

conservative than Franklin and many other phoneticists, and -- we must confess -- not entirely uniform. We feel that words like 'the, that, thee .....' are not really a problem and we are quite comfortable in retaining the 'th-' spelling for the 'th' sound (even when -- as above -- that sound is mildly equivocal); and we make the same decision regarding the '-ng' sound and spelling.

(4) On the other hand, we do favor putting to new use one of the letters Franklin found redundant: 'c' replaces 'ch'. The reason is that 'c' is available and 'ch' is an independent sound and inexplicable in terms of a compound construction. A similar attempt to employ 'q' as the 'sh' sound was carried through much of the first development of Modular English but eventually fell of its own weight. It was abandoned because it gave rise to too many jarring renditions of common words like 'surely' which became 'qirlee', 'mission' became 'miqun', 'she' became 'qe'. All of these are as possible as any other convention and no problem for the complete neophyte learning the language for the first time. For anyone already literate in traditional English, however, they seemed completely repellent and -- on testing -- even ludicrous. Discretion being the better part of valor and being ourselves anxious to make the the Modular English reform palatable to everyone, we abandoned this attempt and abandoned the letter 'q' with it. Our original motivation was in feminist politics and symmetry: it put 'she' as 'qe' symmetrical with 'he'. This experience stands as an object lesson on the hazards of mixed agenda!

(5) The fate of 'x' remains equivocal, but it would seem to be useful in 'fix' for example, rather than the alternative 'fiks' which could be confused with the plural of 'fik'. The example of 'eks'-ample or 'ekz'-ample or 'egz'-ample all seem to indicate a useful job for 'x' and we will retain it. As with so many of Franklin's reforms, its

banishment seems to solve a non-problem while introducing gratuitous complications and confusions.

(6) Franklin's dismissal of 'y' as redundant is surely based on the same notion that sound and name should be identical. Yet anyone who grew up a cowboy would feel deprived of 'yippee' and 'yahoo'; so yeah, y'all, us cowboys gotta job for 'y' and we're gonna keep it.

Other examples of Franklin's reforms illustrated in the poem reproduced by Oswald defy understanding.

(1) Some are inconsistent and illogical. For example the use of '-ii-' for the sound '-ee-' as in the rendering of serene (siriin [4]), pleased (pliiz'd [5]), stream (striim [7]), etc., conflicts with its use in clear (kliir [9]) unless Franklin is trying to dictate a pronunciation foreign to us and, in fact, *impossible* to produce in one syllable consistent with stream.

(2) Some are baffling. Franklin introduces a new letter (here ρ) apparently to express a soft exhaling sound similar to -- but less than -- our 'huh'. Whatever its intended purpose, its appearances in some (sρm (1)), by (bρi [1]), ..., furious (fiurips [4]), ..., and finally bosom (bρzρm [12]) can best be described as consistently gratuitous. They are perhaps intended to convey some subtlety that has been elided in modern speech. Whatever its purpose, we won't copy it. In general, our reforms are vastly more conservative than Franklin's, motivated as we are by the most important concern: that for All Little Children. We can only hope that our attempts succeed to the same universal extent that Franklin's and those of all his successors have failed.

Whatever merit our construction turns out to have beyond those of our predecessors -- and we think our reforms to be incomparably superior -- we can credit it to our one guiding principle: Love All the Little Children.

Sec III.3: Samples of A Modern Phonics.

There have been improvements in phonics over the intervening 2 centuries, and here we give a brief glimpse of the phonics of a contemporary practitioner who will remain mercifully anonymous. We will find significant advances over Franklin, of course; but we still take exception to some of the stratagems. Since 'the proof of the pudding .....' and since no significant number of people have shown any appetite for this particular pudding, we feel no particular need to refute it in all detail. In fact, where this example of modern phonics is easy and obvious it is the same as our reformed Modular English. As with Franklin's original version however, it contains the seeds of its own failure in an overweening cleverness which soon becomes a cloying saccharin cuteness.

This is our reaction especially to the use of accent-symbols (as in French) to refine particular pronunciations. An artificially easy example -- which we specifically avoid -- would be to use the unadorned vowel to be soft, and the vowel with an overbar to be hard: then 'net' and 'neat' would be rendered 'net' (as ours) but our neet'. Another example, is to indicate (but only sometimes) now silent vowels by a period: 'realized' becomes 'reealiz.d' (compare our 'reealiezd'). We specifically reject economies based on such dualities because the price is non-uniqueness and ambiguity; in the teaching of little children, introducing such alternatives is a breach of faith which has fatal consequences. Better a seemingly awkward rendition of a word than a seemingly elegant rendition which violates the consistency of the rules.

We of course have our own duality -- between the name of a letter and its job. Both however are unique attributes of the symbol and this faithful connection must never be violated. This dual understanding of the alphabet will be the rock solid foundation on which All Little Children can securely construct -- once and for all needs and for all time -- their mastery of the written language. We must never ever violate the trust they put in this foundation; certainly not for the specious purposes of convenience or elegance or cleverness as perceived by hyper-literate adults.

One Example of Modern Phonics:

deer peeter,

report.z ov heet-relaeted deth.z in teksas prompt dhis mesej. i trvst yu and pamela ar wel -- let me noe.

i dremt about dhe tuu ov yu svm mvnth.z agoe aafter a trip tu yael for a konferens. i doen't remember whot woz in dhe dreem bvt it woz sort ov straenj. however, it woz jvst aafter having vizited hgs for lvnch. evrithing iz diferent widh regardz tu dfe diening haul: dhey'v kombien.d brekfast and lvnch and it'z aul self-servis. i saw veri few peepl eeting dhaer. a few new bilding.z hav sprvng vp (dhe konferens woz in wvn ov dhem).

dhe sekond tiem (a few week.z agoe) woz on mi way tu kaep kod. mi phd adviezor had jvst die.d and i woz goeing tu pik vp a manueskript about shanghaineez (chieneez) he had ritn several dekaed.z agoe. dhis woz tu help me widh mi insvlt stvdi (which i'v probabli toeld yu about -- it'z sort of endles i'm afraid, bvt i'm trieing tu get moest ov it finish.d dhis svmer). for svm reezon, no dreem.z about yu dhat tiem.

dhis woz jvst tu fiend out if yu'r svrvieving dhe heet -- bvt dhen, yu may not eevn be in teksas.

best regard.z, robert

On repeated reading, even this phonics has its own appeal, and it is easy to read with little or no practice. However where it's not obvious, it's maddeningly inconsistent, and even gratuitous, to the point of being at least as difficult as what it's intended to replace. In its defense, there are no really challenging words here on which to demonstrate its full potential. But let's look at the merits and defects apparent even in this simple message.

First the merits:

(1) The message is easily deciphered on the very first reading.

(2) Some conventions are apparently so natural, obvious and compelling, that the ones used here are identical to the ones we also adopted from the start. Among these are 'peeter', 'reel', 'relaeted', 'straenj', 'sekond', 'tiem', 'goeing', 'ritn', and 'fiend'.

A prominent inconsistency is a problem that we met and resolved (which is to admit: did not solve!) in the same way:

(1) From the examples 'peeter', 'goeing', 'relaeted' and many others we conclude that a vowel followed by an 'e' should be hard just as 'hate' becomes 'haet'. But then the very first word 'deer' is an exception. It is true that 'deer' is virtually impossible to pronounce in one syllable as 'dee/er', but — for the rules to be consistent and unique which is so essential in elementary education and should be the principal purpose of all these reforms -- that is what we are ordered to do. In fact we also eventually are forced to succumb on this very point, and introduce a second separate and distinct job for '-ee-' as in 'deer', 'fear', 'mere', etc.

(2) Next, and completely unacceptable in our opinion, no sooner do we adjust to 'v' replacing 'o' in 'svm mvnth' (obviously rendering 'some month') and the similar 'u' in 'jvst' (for 'just'), than we find 'hav sprvng vp' and 'svrvieving'. It is possible to construct a rule to cover these cases but it can not be simple because the 'u' sound in survive is different from the 'u' sound in some, month, sprung, and up. This is a is a serious obstruction

for beginning spellers, just the arbitrary rule we're trying to eliminate. What are All Little Children to think and remember?

(3) Then we find the sequence 'agoe aafter a trip'. Three identical uses of 'a' with what? perhaps a typographical error. All is forgiven.

(4) The 'th' sound is rendered -- for no conceivable reason, and with no resulting economy -- as 'dh' in 'the', 'this', and 'that' but as 'th' in 'month' and 'everything'. Is this a 'distinction without a difference' like Franklin tried to enforce between hard and soft 'th', or is it another oversight? If the former, then it is just another hidden booby-trap for All Little Children. If the latter, then missionaries can be forgiven for only so many lapses in their espousal of their 'true faith'.

(5) We find multiple uses for 'i' including: the hard personal pronoun 'I' rendered as 'i', then the hard 'i' in 'dining' requiring an immediately following 'e' as in 'diening'; the soft 'i' in 'trip', etc., but the unaccompanied and unadorned 'i' in 'evrithing' -- explainable as an elision in some accents, perhaps -- but then again in 'veri' as a hard 'e' sound, and soon in 'mi' as a hard 'i' sound. This is an unresolved – in fact, an unacknowledged -- difficulty. But pressing on:

(6) We find 'even' as 'eevn' but 'reason' as 'reezon'. Why not 'reezn'?

(7) We find 'tuu' for 'too' and 'tu' for 'to' and who knows what or why for 'two'. We must do better and we will.

Other changes we find to be somewhat gratuitous.

(1) There never was a difficulty with the strictly observed rule of capitalizing the first word of a sentence. We find no reason or advantage in abandoning this rule.

(2) Similarly, capitalization of names is a nice courtesy and gives a small emphasis when written.

(3) There are capitalizations which are useful: the first person singular pronoun 'I' is as economical as it can be.

Its pronunciation is the same as the name of the letter 'i'. In a name such as 'Italy' it will be pronounced in our reformed modular English like the defining 'sit', etc. At the start of a sentence such as the preceding one, the word 'In' again is pronounced like the defining 'sit'.

(4) Another convention crops up with silent vowels (see (6) above) when making plurals: among many examples we find 'dreem.z' for 'dreams'. In our modular English we adopt 'dreemz'. We do not want to hear a rationalization of the '.' even if there is one. Such gratuitous conventions supported by arbitrary rules are just what we are trying to eliminate from the written English language.

A slightly more recent example from the same author has a few changes but no real signs of progress, in fact quite the contrary. This excerpt looks like it came right out of a copy of *Mein Kampf* or -- perhaps less threatening -- from an episode of the TV comedy series Stalag XVII:

A Modified Version of Phonics By the Same Author:

''......ve vil hav a reli sensibl riten styl. Zer vil be no mor trubls or difikultis and evrivun vil find it ezi tu understand ech ozer. Ze drem vil finali kum tru.!!!!''

All these examples illustrate the significant advance in philosophy and priorities of our reforms -- intended to produce a uniquely consistent *modular* written version of the spoken English language -- compared to the reforms of doctrinaire phonetics.

It's always easy to criticize, so let's see what we can do. I promise you that it will be a gigantic improvement over what we have seen so far. The critical guiding principles responsible for the improvement are these:

(1) Consistency and uniqueness.
(2) Create no problems where none exist.

(3) Love All Little Children above everything else.

One thing we will find as we proceed is new respect for our predecessors: there *are* difficulties which *we too* have been unable to eradicate from the language.

CHAPTER FOUR:
ELEMENTS OF MODULAR ENGLISH.

Sec IV.1: Introductory Remarks.

After all the preparatory exhortations, it's somewhat embarrassing to finally reveal how simple and obvious Modular English really is. The first generation of changes are -- rightly so -- almost childlike in their ease of comprehension. We will first define the dominant role assigned to each of the 26 letters of the traditional English alphabet. We keep them all but one, abandoning 'q', and all their usual names. But then the plot begins to unfold.

First we assign each letter a fundamental role defined by its use in simple single syllable words. Even at this elementary stage there are choices involved, which we hope to have made in an optimal way. These choices will be the basic contract among the users of the language and we must try to honor this contract.

Admittedly, we soon meet difficulties and awkward constructions: the language is always a work in progress. We can only hope that in this work, and in this progress, the revisions and improvements are made with the interests of All Little Children kept in mind. We hope that future language innovators will curb all pseudo-sophistication and smart-aleck cleverness masquerading as intelligence. Such anti-social obstructions to the new Modular English language would include resorting to the former (i.e., now present, but soon to be archaic) language in order to show-off a falsely presumed superior and elitist form of literacy; or willy-nilly carrying modular reforms to extremes -- one of which is to ascribe vowel sounds to consonants in order to compactify words into a 'bfstk' parody of phonetics completely at odds with the extremely rational and orderly principles of Modular English.

The fundamental elements of the Modular English written language introduced in this chapter are sufficient to solve over 80% of the eventualities arising in even the most complex spelling constructions. There are wrinkles in the fabric of this first generation Modular English, some of which require extensions of our basic contract. We can't anticipate all the difficulties, but we do propose pragmatic solutions for a few of the most obvious ones.

One of our founding principles has to be compromised from the start. The doctrine of uniqueness is abandoned immediately in the *dual tasks* assigned to the letter 'e' which -- in Modular English as in traditional English -- is the 'big brother' of vowels with two functions: it has the usual soft vowel sound defined by its use in a common single syllable word like 'bet'; but it also has the function -- as before, but now mandatory and universal -- of silently signaling the hard vowel pronunciation of the _now immediately_ preceding vowel, for example as before in 'beet' for 'beet' but now also in 'boet' for 'boat'; and -- most especially definitive of this difference between the reformed and the traditional spelling -- as in 'raet' for 'rate', where the affected 'a' *immediately* precedes the modifying 'e'. Enforcing this rule -- which we will (almost!) *universally* and *without exception* – has obvious reverberations in the homonym 'beat' and the di-syllabic word 'poet' which will be dealt with in separate ways to be discussed later.

A separate situation occurs in 'deer' which is a lasting problem for which we have no really attractive solution (a shortcoming shared with all phonetic versions of English).

But now at last we cut to the chase.

Sec IV.2: Fundamental Elements of Modular English.

The fundamental task performed by the vowels 'a, e, i, o, u' (Note: not including 'y') is defined to be the soft vowel sound appearing in (my pronunciation of) selected simple single-syllable words:

(1) 'a' as in 'bat', 'sat', 'fat', 'rat', 'ran', 'fan', 'ban', 'man', and so on.
(2) 'e' as in 'ten', 'men', 'den', 'net', 'set', 'let', 'bet', 'bed', and so on.

(3) 'i' as in 'tin', 'bit', 'sit', 'fit', 'bin', 'kid', 'rid', 'rim', and so on.

(4) 'o' as in 'tot', 'rot', 'lot', 'not'; but <u>NOT</u> 'ton' or 'son'. For 'or', see later.

(5) 'u' as in 'run', 'sun', 'fun', 'bun'; 'hut' and 'but', but <u>NOT</u> 'put'.

These usages will also define the role of certain consonants which we characterize as *hard*. These unequivocally will include (b, d, k, l, m, n, p, t). The others '*soft*' consonants (c, f, g, h, j, q, r, s, v, w, x, y, z) require some choices which we will expand upon individually and in order in the next section on the alphabet.

Other constructions are not always unequivocal. Examples sometimes occur when one or more soft consonants bracket a vowel. These include:

(1) The 'a' in 'far' might be considered distinct from that in 'fat' and there is a temptation to distinguish it by a construction like 'fahr'. This is an arguable conclusion because both soft consonants 'f' and 'r' involve an extra exhalation which is compounded in 'far'. There is a hint of this in 'fat' but, peculiarly, not in an initial 'r' as in 'rat'. We will not succumb to this temptation to ascribe different degrees of 'airiness' to such vowels but make the burden implicit in the soft consonants. The resulting economies will be widespread,

(2) The 'e' in 'fer(ry)' is similar and will not be distinguished. This actually accomplishes a nice compactification of the homonyms 'fair' and 'fare' into 'fer', as also 'ferry' and 'fairy' into 'feree'; also 'veree' and 'heree' different from 'hiree'. Not a terribly pretty sight. 'Fear' is a problem as we saw with 'dear' and 'deer'. We lean more and more to rendering them as 'feer' and 'deer' and depending on the impossibility of pronouncing them as dictated to soften the hardness of the '-ee-' to something closer to common usage. This

47

will remain a conflict with 'feed' and 'deed' but it's the best we have done so far.

(3) The 'i' in 'fir' remains and 'fur' becomes 'fir'; and 'wonder' becomes 'wundir', or even the extreme 'wundr' is completely understandable as is 'wundird' or 'wundrd'. The last is perilously close to 'bfstk' we must admit.

(4) The 'o' in 'for' remains and 'fore' and 'four' (preferably *always* replaced by the numeral '4') both become 'for'; 'or', 'ore', AND 'oar' will be 'or'.

(5) The 'u' in 'fur' is abandoned in favor of 'i' as in (3); but the 'u' in 'put' becomes 'puht', and 'putt' becomes 'put' just as 'butt' becomes 'but'.

We have already mentioned the accompanying silent 'e' to signal the hard vowel sound:

(1) 'rate' becomes 'raet'; 'ate' and 'eight' (again preferably '8') become 'aet'.

(2) As above, 'replete' becomes 'reepleet', 'very' becomes 'veree', 'onomatopoeia' becomes 'onamatapeea' resisting any temptation to end in '-ya'.

(3) 'site', 'sight' AND 'cite' become 'siet'. 'Diet' becomes 'dieit' (not -- by fiat -- 'dieet', which is possible and understandable and acceptable and depends on a subtlety of accent).

(4) 'poet' becomes 'poeit' because 'poetess' is pronounced 'poe-it-ess'; but because 'poetic' is pronounced 'poe-et-ic', it should become 'poeetik'. (Note: we replace the hard 'c' by 'k'.)

(5) 'use' the noun becomes 'ues'; 'use' the verb becomes 'uez'. 'Diurnal' becomes (without the hyphens) 'die-ir-nl' ('ur' as in 'fir') losing its lexicographic connection to the Latin. 'Diuretic' is a new problem and can be elided as above, or written (without the hyphens) as 'die-ue-retik' to retain its urinary connections; or perhaps better as 'die-yir-etik'. Then with 'urine' as 'yirin' the problems are eliminated with 'dieyiretik', all in agreement with my old dictionary.

This is just a brief first introduction to the fundamental elements of Modular English. Everything is determined by the little words. To quote Winston Churchill: ''I love words; and the words I love best are the little words.'' Now we will have vastly more reason to love these little words. They will determine everything we do to make the Modular English written language simple to learn, to read, and especially to spell. There will be subtleties at the 10-20% level which require going beyond these simple dictates to take care of especially difficult issues. These amount really to almost ignorable embellishments; sometimes simple agreements and conventions to eliminate ambiguities, but some actual real difficulties *have* defied simple solutions. We are stopped here eventually by the Third Law of Thermodynamics: The price of perfection, like that of reaching absolute zero temperature, is infinite.

The next section will take us literally from ''a,A to z,Z'' through the alphabet, specifically defining the role of each of the 26 familiar letters. There is usually only one such role; and only one letter -- c -- gets a new and unique assignment to express the sound 'ch'; and only one letter -- q – gets eliminated from the new alphabet. The letters 'e' and 'h' are quite exceptional in their weighty assignments.

Sec IV.3: The Old Alphabet in the New Modular English.

a, A -- (1) has the soft pronunciation as in 'mat', the hard pronunciation as in 'mate' now to be spelled 'maet'. The name of the letter remains as traditionally pronounced hard 'a' now written 'ae'. When appearing in isolation as the indefinite article 'a' it will always have the soft pronunciation as in 'bat'.

(2) The hard accentuated version of the article and the name of the letter are now to be faithfully rendered as 'ae'.

(3) Peculiar constructions such as 'wait' and 'weight' become 'waet'. 'Eight' is preferably replaced by the numeral '8' avoiding pomposity in favor of simplicity and directness. 'Ate' becomes 'aet'.

(4) The long soft 'a' as in 'father', sometimes rendered 'fawther', will become 'fothir' following the chain of definition from 'pot' to 'potir', 'dot' to 'dotir', from 'sot' to 'slot' to 'sloth', then from 'bot-' (not 'boet-') to 'both-' (not 'boeth-') to 'bother' (with an undifferentiated but here harder 'th') now as 'bothir', and finally to 'fothir'.

(5) Another job for 'a' is preceding 'r' as defined in 'bar', 'tar', 'hard', etc., all unchanged; so 'are' becomes 'ar'   As explained above, this avoids the too breathy construction 'fahr' but probably only postpones the too succinct – in our already reactionary view -- 'Toys-R-Us' rendering of 'are' and 'ar'.

b, B -- (1)   has the unequivocal hard sound as in 'bat'.   The name remains unchanged and is spelled 'bee'.

(2) The subtle silent 'b' as in 'subtle' and 'dumb' is eliminated. The double 'bb' as in 'stubborn' no longer occurs.

(3) The false economy -- succumbed to in some extreme forms of phonetics apparently seeking to optimize compactification at the expense of consistency -- to employ an isolated 'b' as the word 'be' (now 'bee') will be avoided. This illustrates a desirable principle of our Modular English, that *syllables* require *explicit vowels*. An exception can and will occur where elision weakens the definition of the syllable. We

might well anticipate with a liberal and permissive attitude that common usage will be the determining factor, and it will be useless to try to defend these weak outposts of the written language.

c, C -- is the one exceptional letter which will be assigned a completely new task and preferably even a new name. The former uses:

(1) where the soft 'c' indicates an extremely delicate sibilant 's' as in 'advice' will be replaced universally by an 's', so 'advice' becomes 'advies' (and 'advise' becomes 'adviez'); and

(2) where the hard 'c' is interchangeable with a 'k' as in 'practical' will be replaced universally by a 'k' so 'practical' becomes 'praktikal'; and

(3) where the silent 'c' as in 'tack' will be eliminated so 'tack' becomes 'tak'.

(4) Rather than dropping the symbol 'c' from the alphabet we will rehabilitate it to replace the compound (and phonetically independent) sound now expressed by 'ch'; so 'such' becomes 'suc', 'check' becomes 'cek'.

(5) A glance at a dictionary reveals a snake-pit of pronunciations of the compound 'ch': chagrin, chain, chair, chaise, chameleon, chamois, champagne, chancre, chandelier, chant, chaos, chap, character, charade, charlatan, charm, Charon, Charybdis, chasm, chassis, chaste, cheap, check, cheer, chela, chemistry, Cheops, cheroot, chi, chic, Chinook, chiropractor, choir, choke, cholera, Christ .... Had enough? Still think we should let well enough alone? Still think the ability to read and spell is an indicator of anything better than a slavish (i.e., weakly submissive, lacking originality and independence, servile, cringing, groveling, abject) mentality anxious (and -- we must admit -- able) to

51

memorize uncritically anything and everything to please higher authority?

(6) It will be useful in the new Modular English to pronounce the name of the letter 'c, C' as 'chee' as in 'cheech and chong' now to be spelled 'cee' as in 'ceec and cong'.

d, D -- (1) is similar to 'b', and has the clear-cut task defined by the fundamental mono-syllabic words 'bid', 'bed', 'dip'; the name is unchanged and will be spelled 'dee'.

(2) The only caveat is similar to that accompanying 'b': 'd' does not independently imply a separate syllable as in the phonetic inconsistency involved in the abbreviation of 'decide' as 'dsied';

(3) in Modular English 'decide' becomes 'desied'. The elision of the first syllable could arguably lead to the phonetic 'd'cide' now as 'disied' but we continue to frown on 'dsied' although this is probably a lost cause. Spelling can only be determined by speech, Jonathan Swift to the contrary notwithstanding.

(4) To represent the past tense of a verb, 'd' will be sufficient in 'realized' which becomes 'reealiezd', but not in 'decided' which becomes 'desieded', or the variants mentioned above.

(5) The double 'd' as in 'riddle' is eliminated and 'riddle' becomes -- arguably -- 'ridel'.

(6) An issue separate from the function of 'd' arises here: the very legitimate arguments for 'ridil' and 'ridul', and maybe best of all the tempting form 'ridl' for the elided last syllable must be considered in a broader light: it is probably a lost cause -- once the floodgates of change have been opened -- to take a too conservative stance, and the form 'ridl' with the past tense 'ridld', although seemingly radical, is probably inevitable. These are radical steps which we take with some

personal reluctance, as if we are being dragged along by the actual use of the language to make it simpler and simpler. There is the incredible feeling of starting an avalanche which is going to take on a huge momentum of its own as it races down from the icy peaks of academe to the populous waiting in the valley. All we can do is to follow our primary fundamental principle of consistency wherever it leads, always remembering to love All Little Children.

e, E -- (1)   as discussed already -- and as before -- has a dual role, as a vowel and as an enforcer of the hard pronunciation of all vowels including itself.

(2) The fundamental soft pronunciation is defined by the words 'pet' and 'bed' and so on.

(3) The hard pronunciation defined by 'beet' and 'neat' is indicated universally by 'e' as a vowel followed immediately by 'e' as the enforcer, so we get 'beet' still as 'beet', but 'neat' as 'neet', 'replete' as reepleet' and so on.

(4) The name of the letter remains the same spelled 'ee'.

(5) The example 'beat' becoming 'beet' indicates the fate of all homonyms in Modular English. As in speech, written homonyms will be distinguished from each other *only* by their context and *not* by their spelling. As mentioned before, fewer than 0.1% of English words are homonyms so this is not a significant problem.

f, F -- (1)   still named 'eff' and pronounced as defined in 'fit', 'fan' and so on.

(2) 'f' is a soft consonant with an airy, breathy sound which will *not* be made explicit as already discussed for the somewhat subtle distinction between the degree of exhalation used, and the resulting pronunciation of 'fit' and 'bit'. A mild temptation arises to put the onus on the 'i' and write 'fit' as

'fiht' or perhaps more logically as 'fhit' to distinguish the breathy sound from the defining word 'bit'. We put the onus on the soft consonant, so the breathy sound is implicit in the 'f' (and later in the other similarly breathy soft consonants 'w', 'h', 'r', and in the exceptional but similar 'y').

(3) So 'fit' and 'bit', 'rat' and 'bat', even 'far' and 'bar' where 'bar' *defines* the 'ar' sound.

g, G -- (1) will have a dual role. Its defining role as an independent hard consonant will be that in 'get' and 'bag' and so on.

(2) Its role in such words as 'gentle' will be assigned to 'j'.

(3) Obscure roles like 'high' will be abolished entirely (in this case 'high' and 'hie' AND 'hi' all become 'hie').

(4) Its name can usefully be pronounce with the hard 'g' as 'gee' as in 'geese' rather than the former 'jee' as in 'gee whiz!' the mild oath, a variant of 'Jesus!'.

(5) An important role for 'g' is that in the combination 'ng' as defined in 'sing', 'singing', 'wing', 'running', 'Bennington', etc., which will be retained; but must be distinguished from the pronunciation of 'bingo' which will require 'binggo'.

(6) Double 'gg' as in 'gagging' will be eliminated in favor of 'gaging'. This can no longer be confused with 'gauge' -- sometimes written 'gage' -- which will become 'gaej' leading to 'gauging' or 'gaging' -- which previously had to be distinguished from 'gagging' -- now becoming 'gaejing'.

h, H -- (1) still named 'aitch' or now 'aec'. It has multiple traditional assignments:

(1) the first assignment is as a soft vowel in isolation defined by the fundamental mono-syllabic words 'hit', 'hat', 'hot' which do not change, and now 'hie' and 'hee' which did;

(2) the second assignment is in the combination 'th' as defined in such simple words as 'bath' which does not change, and 'both' which does change for a previous reason to 'boeth'.

(3) There is different harder pronunciation of 'th' as in 'thy' which Franklin chose to express as a new letter. We won't complicate matters like that. The spoken language will dictate usage, the written language will follow as faithfully as possible but in this case only suggesting the emphasis. Give us an A-. One 'th' will have to fit all. Hopefully we will never be concerned about contiguities with 'thie thie'.

(4) Other usages in obscure places like 'graph', 'might', 'rough', and 'thorough' will be abolished in favor of 'graf', 'miet', 'ruf', and 'thiroe' ('ir' as in 'fir') in my accent or possibly 'thoroe' in some others, but obvious in each case.

(5) Other uses of 'h' have been contemplated above as in 'fahr' for an emphasized exhalation in this case. We avoided this by putting the burden on the two soft consonants, and will continue to try -- at the very least -- to avoid such complications. None the less, 'h' is a 'bic'.

(6) The extra exhalation distinguishing the 'u' in 'put' from that in 'but' will be expressed with an explicit 'h' as 'puht', leaving 'put' rhyming with 'but' and replacing 'putt'. This construction also appears in 'buhk', 'tuhk', 'thuh', and the colloquially elided 'to' becomes 'tuh' as in 'goeing tuh town'.

(7) A further use for 'h' has finally and after much agonizing been reintroduced in the compound 'sh' as in 'she' appearing in many places like 'atenshun' or inevitably 'atenshn' for 'attention', 'konekshn' (NOT 'konexn') for 'connection',

'dimenshn' for 'dimension' and so on -- comparable to 'th' compound;

(8) and in the similar 'zh' as in 'vizhun' or – growing more attractive by the moment -- 'vizhn' for 'vision', 'desizhn' or its variants already mentioned of 'disizhn' or 'dsizhn' for 'decision'.

The twisted trail that led back to these usages is discussed at great length in the subsection for the letter **q,Q.**

i, I -- (1)   The name is pronounced 'ie', and

(2) the soft pronunciation is defined by 'bid', 'dim', 'sit', etc., words with hard consonants.

(3) the possibly subtly different pronunciation with soft consonants is defined by 'fit' and 'rid' but 'fir'.

(4) The hard pronunciation is achieved as usual with an immediately following 'e', so: 'mite' and 'might' become 'miet', 'tire' becomes 'tieir', 'hired' becomes 'hieird'. Here again there is an argument for 'tier' which would put the 'ir' sound defined by 'fir' either entirely on the 'r' in contradiction with the pronunciation of 'r' defined by 'rid', or the 'e' would be required to do double duty as an enforcer in 'ie' *and* as a vowel in 'er'. The first explanation would cause reverberations in 'fir'; the second in 'ferry' but more importantly would destroy the universal integrity of the enforcer role of 'e'. Our choice avoids both conflicts at the small price of the explicit 'ir' syllable.

(5) Finally we come to the most singular task of 'i' and that is -- capitalized -- as the personal pronoun 'I'. We advocate replacing it with 'Ie' in accord with the traditional pronunciation and the reformed spelling. The extra 'e' might seem a burden to some but is similar to the French 'je' sometimes elided to 'j''; and is more compact than the

German 'ich'. Neither the French nor the German capitalizes this pronoun except at the beginning of a sentence, but I like the capital and advocate keeping it.

j, J -- (1)   retains its traditional name now spelled 'jae' and

(2) its traditional pronunciation defined by 'jab', 'jet', etc.; and

(3) now assumes this same task from 'g' in words like 'giant' now 'jieint', and 'gentle' now 'jentl'; 'gigantic' becomes 'jiegantik'.

(4) For some reason, 'j' is a letter with unusual integrity, singleness of purpose, and lack of ambiguity. The rare exceptions like 'Jugoslavia' and 'joie de vivre' seem to be unassimilated foreign words.

k, K -- (1)   retains its traditional name now spelled 'kae' and

(2) its traditional pronunciation defined by 'kid', 'ken', etc.; but

(3) now assumes the same task in situations previously taken by a hard 'c' such as 'cad' now 'kad', and similarly for 'accord' now 'akord', 'practical' now 'praktikal' or 'praktikul' or finally probably best to submit and accept 'praktikl' (Why be the last rat on this sinking ship?); but also

(4) now assumes the same or similar task previously taken by the combination 'qu' with silent 'u' as in the archaic British 'cheque' become the American 'check' and now the Modular English 'cek', remembering the elimination of silent 'c' and the new assignment of 'c' for the old 'ch' sound. Another slightly more complicated assignment for 'k' will be

(5) to replace the 'qu' as in 'quite' and 'quiet' with 'kw' giving 'kwiet' and 'kwieit'. Here the choice 'it' for the final syllable -- although somewhat arbitrary --agrees with the

similar choices made in 'poet' as 'poeit' and 'diet' as 'dieit'. This replaces the whole 'q'-section of the dictionary in an obvious way already indicated for practically every word which is accompanied there by the prescription 'qu-' equals 'kw-'. Rare exceptions are 'queue' now 'kue', quetzal, Quezon, Quito, qui vive, and Quixote but 'quixotic' pronounced there and at last now spelled here as 'kwiksotik'. There is no difficulty in the Modular English spelling of the exceptions, and certainly no lexicographic reason not to do so because quetzal and Quito are Spanish renderings of Aztec and Inca names, and Quezon a Spanish rendering of a Philippine name.

l, L -- (1) retains its name 'el' and also

(2) its pronunciation defined as in 'let', 'lot'.

(3) All double 'll' constructions are abolished in favor of single 'l': so 'tell' becomes 'tel', 'fill' becomes 'fil'; and 'wonderful' becomes 'wundirfuhl' (with a grand total of 3 changes and one eliminated ambiguity (the final '-l' or '-ll') at the cost of one exercise of judgement -- 'wundir' or 'wundr'), 'fulfill' becomes 'fuhlfil', 'beautiful' -- already reduced to one 'l', an inconsistency in the traditional spelling as annoying as the redundancy of 2 'l's -- becomes 'buetifuhl'. 'Miller' becomes 'milir' and 'miler' (as in 4-minute miler) becomes 'mielir'.

(4) All silent 'l's are abolished, so 'calm' becomes 'kom', 'psalm' becomes 'som'.

(5) A dilemma arises in words like 'double' or 'handle'. The question is whether and how to make the second elided syllable explicit. Should it be 'handil' or 'handel' or 'handul'? We take our lead from 'doubling' and 'handling' and are slowly learning our lesson in choosing none of the above, but rather the maximally contracted and simplified 'dubl' and 'handl'. We have resolved the dilemma in the

58

way that time and use surely would eventually, but we anticipate endless argument over this and many other choices that simply *have* to be made. Again we refer to the fundamental principle of uniqueness, consistency, and here simplicity. Love All Little Children.

m, M -- (1) retains its name 'em' and

(2) its pronunciation as defined in 'mit', 'dim', 'mum', and so on.

(3) All double 'm's are eliminated, so 'comment' becomes 'koment' as already given in my old dictionary to explain the pronunciation.

(4) Where formerly supported by silent companions, 'm' will now stand alone like 'pom' replacing 'palm', 'dum' replacing 'dumb', and 'dam' replacing 'damn' and now not distinguished in writing from its homonym.

(5) As we found with the letter 'j', 'm' is a letter practically devoid of ambiguity or corruption.

n, N -- (1) retains its name 'en' and

(2) its pronunciation as defined in 'bin', 'ban', 'den', 'net', and so on.

(3) All double 'n's and silent 'n's are eliminated; so 'spinning' becomes 'spining', 'dinning' becomes 'dining' but 'dining' becomes 'diening'; 'damn' becomes 'dam' but 'damnation' becomes 'damnaeshun', after resolution of the 'sh' sound.

(4) The same dilemma of elided syllables that we encountered with 'l' also occurs frequently with 'n'. We will resolve it in the same spineless way, again anticipating the irresistible forces of time and tide. So 'burden' becomes 'birdn' and 'burdening' becomes 'birdning'.

o, O -- currently has a multiplicity of tasks illustrated by the traditional pronunciation of the elementary words 'not', 'both', 'note', 'moat', 'to' and 'too' AND 'two', 'or', 'more', 'book', 'spoof', and 'moor' and surely more which we will have to rationalize. To begin

(1) the letter 'o' retains its name 'oe' and

(2) the soft sound defined in the common words 'tot', 'dot', 'bob' (but not 'ton'), 'sob', 'rot' (but not for) etc.

(3) The hard pronunciation is enforced universally with the immediately following 'e' as in 'toe' which is unchanged; 'slow' becomes 'sloe', 'owe' becomes 'oe', 'mow' becomes 'moe', 'bow in her hair' becomes 'boe in hir her', 'bow and arrow' becomes 'boe and eroe', etc.

(4) A different soft sound defined in the combination '-or' from the fundamental 'or' and 'for', so 'more' becomes 'mor', 'oar' and 'ore' are not distinguished from the fundamental defining 'or', 'horticulture' becomes 'hortikulcir' or inevitably 'hortikulcr', 'wore' and 'war' and become 'wor'; 'whore' becomes 'hor', 'boar' and 'bore' become 'bor'.

(5) The variety of double 'o's must be resolved. In our pronunciation 'took', 'book' and 'put' are similar. The added exhalation in 'put' as compared to the standard soft 'u' defined by 'but' is accomplished by the Modular English assignment 'uh'. So consistent with 'put' becoming 'puht', 'took' becomes 'tuhk', 'book' becomes 'buhk', 'look' becomes 'luhk' (and 'luck' becomes 'luk').

(6) The other double 'o' as in 'proof' and 'spoof', 'spool', 'boot' and 'boo', and hence 'too', will be retained. Depending on your accent, 'roof' will be 'roof' to rhyme with 'proof' or 'ruhf' as in 'puht'.

(7) This gives rise to another dilemma: If we accept the double 'o' spelling for 'too', what becomes of the homonyms 'to' and 'two'? 'To' is commonly elided to a weak 'tuh' as in 'go t' town'; 'two' is a pretentious way of writing the numeral '2'. These are elemental words in the language, but if we are going to clean up the mess we must be consistent. For this reason we compact 'to' and 'too' AND 'two' into the single 'too' in formal speech and the vernacular 'tuh' or even t' when describing normal elided conversation. More arguments! But we must fight for consistency. What's the old saying? "Consistency is the hob-goblin of little minds." But that is precisely the problem we are facing. We are designing a written language as much as possible like the spoken language for the sake of All Little Children. They are All Little Children but their minds are not little. Nonetheless, more than a third of them have difficulty coping with the *multiplicity* of possible choices to be made at every juncture of the language. Consistency, uniqueness, a clear specific path through the maze is what we seek.

p, P -- is a quite unequivocal hard consonant with a number of esoteric irregular but traditional uses as in 'graph' and 'psalm'.

(1) It will retain its name 'pee', and

(2) its pronunciation as defined in the fundamental monosyllabic words such as 'top', 'pep', etc.

(3) All double 'p' constructions will be abolished, so 'pepper' becomes 'pepir', 'slippery' becomes 'slipiree' or maybe even 'slipree', and so on. We feel no obligation to define the spelling of this slippery word in any precise or authoratative way by inventing some rule to cover it. It is just this doctrinaire, dictatorial, absolutely fascistic attitude about the sanctity of an official spelling that has to be changed in order to make the written English Language more user friendly and less destructive to the enthusiasm for learning which every little child brings to the first day of school.

(4) All silent 'p's are dropped, so 'pseudo-' becomes 'soodoe-', 'psychiatrist' becomes 'siekieatrist' rather than the possible 'suhkieatrist' to retain the connection to 'psyche' pronounced and now finally now spelled 'siekee', and pterodactyl, and Ptolemy, and ptomaine, and only a few others.

(5) The usage 'ph' will be replaced by 'f' so that at last 'phonetic' becomes 'foenetik', and 'prophets' become 'profits' at some loss -- or better 'profets' in which case there is no loss.

q, Q -- All the traditional uses of the letter 'q' have been reassigned to 'k' where they have always rationally belonged. The symbol 'q' is now free either for discard as Franklin proposed, or for reassignment. We at first tried to introduce a mixed and completely irrelevant feminist agenda by suggesting that:

(1) 'q' be assigned the presently compound sound 'sh' and the new name 'qee' pronounced as in the old spelling 'she'.

(2) The transformation of the whole 'sh-' subsection of the dictionary followed easily.

(3) With this assignment, the third person singular pronouns masculine 'hee, hiz, him' and feminine 'qee, qiz, qim' forms became fully symmetric rather than the old 'she, her(s), her' which would have become 'shee, hir(z), hir'. The feminine (-ist?) form might still be viewed as being somewhat derivative, but the attempt 'qee, qir(z), qir' immediately involved 'qir' the Modular English form (in this attempted version) of the old 'sure'.

(4) Other 'sh' sounds were easily transformed as 'sugar' became 'quhgir', 'discussion' became 'diskuqun' or even 'diskuqn', 'attention' became 'atenqun' or 'atenqn', 'connection'

became 'konekqun' or 'konekqn' although some might argue for 'konexn'.

This whole new assignment for 'q', although seemingly economical and concise, was literally shocking in its appearance and became increasingly so with further experience. In our extended trial of this new use for 'q' we never were able to get over the discomfort. The final straw came in trying to accommodate the hard 'zh' sound in 'vision' in a way symmetrical with the soft 'sh' sound in 'mission'. The hard 'z' sound in 'his' is expressed symmetrically in Modular English with the soft 's' sound in 'miss' using 'hiz' and 'mis' (recalling that no silent double letters are permitted). Going back to the traditional 'sh' for the soft sound permitted the symmetrical use of 'zh' for the hard sound, and then 'vision' becomes 'vizhn' and 'mission' becomes 'mishn'. There were many other visual difficulties resulting from this attempted use of 'q' such as 'qir' and 'qirlee' for 'sure' and 'surely' (now 'shir' and 'shirlee'), and the unsatisfactory 'disiqn' for 'decision' (now 'disizhn').

We have no doubt that in time we could have made the transition to this new use of 'q' for 'sh' but we would still have been left with the undesirable asymmetrical representation of the 'zh' sound. The compromise resolution to continue to represent these sounds by the compounds 'sh' and 'zh' on equal footing with the compound 'th' has the desired symmetry. Certainly more important, is the value of this compromise in easing the transition from traditional to Modular English for mature readers. The recognition of 'disizhn' and all other such words in their Modular English form is immediate.

There is no further use for 'q' and -- as Franklin initially proposed -- it will be dropped from the alphabet.

r, R -- the soft consonant already much discussed

(1) has the primary hard pronunciation defined by the fundamental monosyllabic words 'red', 'rob', 'run', etc.; but also

(2) a softer breathier pronunciation defined by a second tier of fundamental monosyllabic words 'far', 'bar', etc.; from which

(3) we write the name of the letter 'r' as 'ar' rhyming with 'bar'.

(4) The pronunciation with other vowels has already been defined by 'far', 'for', 'fir', 'fur' becomes 'fir', 'fer' as in 'ferry' so 'fare' and 'fair' become 'fer', 'bare' and 'bear' become 'ber', 'fairy' and 'ferry' become 'feree', 'very' becomes 'veree', and many more.

(5) 'Fear', 'near', 'beer', 'dear' and 'deer' and even 'ear' are all rendered with '-eer'.

(6) Double 'r's are eliminated so 'barrel' becomes 'berel', 'error' becomes 'eror'. The pronunciation *and* spelling of 'err' (sometimes rhyming with the definitive 'fir') will be standardized to 'er' as in 'eror'.

(7) Silent appendages to final 'r's like the 'e' in 'torture' will be dropped of course, and 'torture' becomes 'torcir'.

(8) Final syllables formed with '-er', '-ir', etc. do not seem to be elided like those with '-en', etc. So 'deader' becomes 'dedir' but 'deaden' becomes 'deden' or -- depending on accent and emphasis -- 'dedn'. It is inevitable that such elisions are going to overtake any decreed spelling, and it's clear that not much is lost.

s, S -- a soft consonant (1) with the traditional name 'es'; and

(2) the pronunciation defined by 'sit', 'sun', etc., a soft sibilant sound distinguished from a hard abrupt but similar sound

rendered by 'z' as in the difference between 'ass' and 'as' which now become 'as' and 'az'.

(3) Even softer, more sibilant sounds like 'ice' previously expressed by a soft 'c' are now represented by 's' with 'c' renamed and reassigned (see above); so 'ice' and 'nice' and 'advice' are now 'ies', 'nies' and 'advies', and 'advise, adviser, advised' become 'adviez, adviezir, adviezd' but 'advisedly' becomes 'adviezedlee'.

(4) Double 's's are dropped, so 'scissors' becomes 'sizirz', exactly as prescribed in my old 1952 Thorndike-Barnhart Dictionary.

(5) The compound 'sh' retains its traditional role as in 'she' which becomes 'shee'; and replaces similar soft 'sh' sounds previously rendered by '-sion' and '-tion' which now become '-shn' (or possibly the accentuated forms with a vowel) as in 'mishn' for mission', 'dikshn' (but not 'dixn') for 'diction'. The harder 'zh' sound of 'vision' is made explicit with the compound 'zh' as in 'vizhn'.

t, T -- (1) retains its name now 'tee' and

(2) its hard consonant pronunciation is defined in such elementary words as 'sit', 'ten', etc.

(3) 't' has the important compound role -- which we retain -- in the 'th' of 'thin' which will be undistinguished from the slightly different 'th' in 'then'. As mentioned this makes 'thy' and 'thigh' both 'thie' to be distinguished in speech by emphasis or accent but in written form only by context.

(4) Double 't's are eliminated so 'tittle' becomes 'titil' but probably not 'titl' because of 'titilaet'. But now 'tattle' would become 'tatl' because of 'tatling' and 'tatler' so here is a slight dichotomy which will have to be tested by time and use. It is clear that there is no need here for any doubt

about either word with either spelling. 'Title' becomes 'tietl' and 'titled' --God help us -- becomes 'tietld'.

(5) The '-shun' construction formerly represented by '-tion' is now assigned uniquely to '-shn' or possibly including the vowel as '-shun' when extra emphasis is desired.

u, U -- (1) retains its rather inappropriate traditional name pronounced 'you' now spelled and pronounced 'ue'; and

(2) its short soft sound as defined in 'sun', 'but', 'nut', etc., so 'luck' becomes 'luk'.

(3) A second traditional longer, softer, and breathier pronunciation occurs in 'put' which will be distinguished as 'puht'. Now 'putt' becomes 'put', and 'book', 'took', 'hook', 'crook', and 'look' have '-ook' replaced by '-uhk'. But 'Luke' and 'pool' (see above) have the double 'o' construction and are now 'Look' and (still) 'pool'.

(4) The hard vowel sound is enforced by 'ue' as in the letter's name and in such words as 'kompuet', 'rebuek' although 'reebuek' also occurs in speech. (If we ever needed to illustrate the ridiculousness of the traditional written English language this single innocuous word 'sp*ee*ch' meaning 'the act of sp*ea*king' says it all. What arbitrary meaningless gratuitous useless confusing trivial maddening inconsistency! Out with it all!). 'Tutor' and 'Tudor' and 'tuber' become either 'tootir' or 'tuetir' or even 'tuetr', and so on, depending on the choice of pronunciation where there seems to be no dominant preference; there then remains an embarrassment with 'tuetoryal'.

v, V -- is a very unequivocal hard consonant and has no changes.
(1) Its name is still 'vee', and

(2) its pronunciation is defined in the simplest usages like 'van', 'vet', 'vat', 'save' now 'saev', 'sieve' now 'siv', and so on.

(3) Examples of its use are 'survive' which becomes 'sirviev'; 'have' which becomes 'hav', and many more.

(4) The archaic and rare 'halve' with a silent 'l' also becomes 'hav', but is usually used as 'halves', 'halved', or 'halving'. In any case, it is just one more homonym which will be distinguished – as in speech -- only by its context.

w, W -- because of its arcane name is a frequent victim of over-zealous phoneticists -- starting with Franklin -- who of course can find no use for it based on the name 'double-you'. (1) We retain the name, and

(2) we find good use for the letter in the traditional tasks defined by the fundamental elementary monosyllabic words 'wen', 'wan', 'wow, 'now', and many others.

(3) We abolish many compound uses such as the 'wh-' in 'which' now 'wic', 'why' now 'wie', 'where' now 'wer', 'what' now 'wut', and

(4) even the 'wh-' in breathier words like 'while' which becomes 'wiel' as does 'wile', 'whey' which -- with 'way' and 'weigh' – becomes 'wae', 'whoa' and 'wo' and 'woe' become 'woe'; but

(5) where used inconsistently is eliminated as in 'who' which becomes 'hoo' as in 'spoof' and 'spook'.

(6) Silent 'w's are eliminated so 'show' becomes 'shoe' and 'shoe' becomes 'shoo', but 'shower' becomes 'showir' as in 'baething' or 'shoeir' as in 'wun hoo shoez shooz'.

x, X -- was dispensed with by Franklin, and certainly is a candidate for reassignment because

(1) its traditional name 'eks' suggests its replacement by the compound 'ks'. One possible task for it would be the sound 'th'. In a fit of conservatism we have retained the 'th' and the 'x'. An argument for the first decision might be to ease the transition by keeping common words somewhat familiar in appearance so 'thuh' suggests 'the' whereas 'xuh' does not. A counter-argument would exist if we had replaced 'she' by 'qee', but recall that attempt was abandoned in favor of just this easing of the transition. An argument for the decision to keep 'x' might be to avoid the radical change between the singular and plural of words like 'duck, ducks' now 'duk, duks' so that when one sees 'fluks' for 'flux' the instinct is to look around for a solitary 'fluk'. Time will tell. In the meantime

(2) we have 'expect' now 'expekt', 'function' now 'funkshn' not 'funxin', 'fluctuate' now 'fluxueaet' or 'fluxooaet' not 'flukshueaet' or 'flukshooaet' and not a pretty sight in any case.

(3) Words beginning with 'x' are rare and better expressed with 'z' from 'xanthous' (yellow) to 'xylophone', but excepting 'X-ray'.

y, Y -- was another candidate for extinction by Franklin because of its uninstructive name.

(1) We retain the name now 'wie' and

(2) the very useful tasks defined by elementary words 'yes', 'yell', 'yak', 'yam', 'yet', 'yen', 'yap', and 'yoyo' now 'yoeyoe';

(3) but not 'why' now 'wie', and not 'by' or 'buy' both now 'bie' as is the prefix 'bi-' now 'bie-'.

(4) In short, the role of 'y' is restricted to that of soft consonant and no longer includes its ambiguous roles as vowel. These

are now taken over by hard 'ie' or 'ee' where required, and very rarely by a soft 'i'. So we have 'sky' becoming 'skie', 'very' and 'vary' becoming 'veree', etc., and 'yttrium' becoming 'itreeum'.

(5) One essential contribution of 'y' as a soft consonant is to modify 'a, e, i, o' soft and hard vowel sounds, and soft 'u' sounds. The obvious exception is because of the redundancy in 'yue-' indistinguishable from 'ue-'. Easy examples are 'yes' still 'yes', 'yawl' now 'yol', 'y'all' also 'yol' perhaps with an apostrophe, 'yodel' now 'yoedl', 'young' now 'yung', and so on. All grateful for their 'y' and a phonetic problem without it.

(6) A special case appears already in 'boy' which must be viewed as unique and definitive. No such situation arises with the other vowels where 'they' becomes 'thae', 'say' becomes 'sae', 'buy' and 'by' become 'bie', etc., all easily realized phonetically. The '-iy' construction is rare. But the '-oy' is unique and awkward if not impossible to achieve in a derivative way, as is the sound when the 'y' precedes any vowel except a hard 'u'.

z, Z -- (1) has the traditional American name pronounced still as 'zee'; with

(2) the traditional pronunciation of hard 's' as defined by such fundamental words as 'jazz' now 'jaz', 'zip', 'zap', 'zot', 'adze' now 'adz', etc.; and in addition

(3) now takes over all those formerly expressed by 's' like 'as' now 'az', 'has' now 'haz', 'regards' now 'reegardz', 'advise' and 'advised' now 'adviez' and 'adviezd', but 'advisedly' now 'advizedlee'. As already mentioned, 'advice' is now 'advies'.

(4) Many words formerly but indefensibly beginning with 'x' now have 'z', as in 'xenophobic' now 'zenafoebik' (where the 'a' is mildly arguable).

(5) Double 'z's are eliminated so 'dazzle' becomes 'dazil' or better 'dazl' as in 'dazling'.

(6) Some 'z' words are unambiguous like 'Zeenoe' and 'zipper' now 'zipir'; 'Zagreb' and 'Zanzibar' remain unchanged; 'zero' is awkward and is solved in an ugly way like 'beer' and 'cheer' as 'zeeroe' which invites pronunciation either as 'zee-roe' or 'zeer-oe'. Again time heals all wounds (an obvious untruth for those wounds which fester and kill).

(7) The readmission of the 'sh' compound allows us to use symmetrically the compound 'zh' for the corresponding hard sound common in 'vizhn' replacing 'vision', 'disizhn' replacing 'decision', and also of use in situations like 'azhir' for 'azure' and 'mezhir' for 'measure'.

Sec IV.4: Looking Ahead.

This brief outline of Modular English gives us sufficient marching orders to jump right in and DO IT!

Rather than try to anticipate every difficulty in advance or in isolation, however, we turn first to the impact of Modular English on reading by examining a few classics of English literature. The suspicion is that Modular English might be at worst inadequate, at best ugly. In the next two chapters we translate into Modular English excerpts from the most beautiful, the most profound, and the most popular English writing.

What we find is at first somewhat strange and surprising. The transposed classics contain neither an indictment nor an emphatic endorsement of the revised written language. The reasons for this will be analyzed further, but in brief they are these:

(1) The classics define the language, and most importantly for us they define the basic elements of Modular English. The result is that translation to the new revised Modular English has relatively little impact on *our* reading.

(2) Great writing -- especially great fiction -- is simple and largely devoid of complicated constructions and pretentious words which are a major target of our spelling reforms.

(3) We are all excellent readers and words leap to mind at the slightest glance. As a result, we can have no appreciation of the pitfalls confronting a 6-10 year old beginning reader. So should we let them wait and struggle and mature and eventually read as we do? We argue NO for the the reason that learning to read and *learning to love reading* must go hand-in-hand, but this is impossible when the path is booby-trapped and land-mined with words like 'thoroughly' and 'rough' and 'cough' and on and on.

(4) Reading is easier than writing. When reading we are reminded of the word as a whole, but are not concerned with all the detailed peculiarities of its spelling. Writing is a much more demanding task. There we have to conjure up the most minute details of every word from memory without any assistance as on a written multiple-choice exam. So writing and spelling are the primary target of spelling reform and we should not expect a comparable impact on reading. Literacy means the ability to read -- in a sense to hear other voices -- *and* to write -- to have a voice of one's own. A person is not complete if he can only hear, but he must also be heard.

CHAPTER FIVE:
MODULAR ENGLISH IN THE CLASSICS.

Sec V.1: Introductory Remarks.

The King James Bible of 1611 is hailed as "the noblest monument of English prose." By its dignity and simplicity it not only conveys a deeply religious feeling and a sense of solemn ritual, but also it has *defined* the English language at its best for all succeeding generations. The epitome of the King James Bible in the Twenty-third Psalm is so apparent that all other versions have been dismissed as superfluous pedestrian pretensions. The question we ask is: can it survive transposition to Modular English? The answer we arrive at is that it can, and surprisingly -- but understandably -- remarkably intact.

On the next page we reproduce the Twenty-third Psalm in Modular English and below in its King James version, although I can't vouch that it is in the old original spelling. Modular English is quite jarring in places, although still readily understandable.

There are some obvious arguments. 'Uv' might be too colloquial for use in a psalm, and 'ov' preferred. Similarly, more formal pronunciations might be preferred accentuating soft or elided syllables into 'eevil', 'pre̱epeṟest', 'anoynte̱st', and 'runne̱th' for example. One does feel grateful for the conservative retention of 'th', and eventually also of the traditional 'sh' and 'zh'. One also has to remember the new 'preper' in place of 'prepare' where we have assigned to '-er-' the tasks formerly belonging to 'ferry' and 'fairy', 'fair' and 'fare', 'air' and 'err', but not 'fir' and its rhymes. It is amusing to note that 'rhymes' was originally 'rimes' and now becomes 'riemz'.

This turns out to be a brain-addling exercise in which repeated scrutiny and experimentation creates doubt in the pronunciation and spelling of words that were never before in question. Furthermore it makes computer spell-checking tedious to the point of useless.

In Modular English, we get:
The King James Version of the 23rd Psalm

Thuh Lord iz mie shepird: Ie shal not wont. (1)
Hee maeketh mee too lie down in green pascirz: (2)
    Hee leedeth mee beesied thuh stil woterz. (3)
Hee reestoreth mie soel: Hee leedeth mee in thuh (4)
    pathz uv riecusnes for Hiz naemz saek. (5)
Yae, thoe Ie wok throo thuh valee uv thuh (6)
    shadoe uv deth, Ie wil feer noe eevl; for Thow (7)
    art with mee: Thie rod and Thie staf thae (8)
    komfirt mee. (9)
Thow preperist a taebl beefor mee in thuh (10)
    prezents uf mien enemeez: Thow anoyntist mie (11)
    hed with oyl; mie kup runith oevir. (12)
Shirlee guhdnes and mirsee shal foloe mee ol (13)
    thuh daez uv mie lief: and Ie wil dwel in thuh (14)
    hows uv thuh Lord forevir. (15)

Compare Traditional English:

The Lord is my shepherd: I shall not want. (1)
He maketh me to lie down in green pastures:(2)
    He leadeth me beside the still waters.(3)
He restoreth my soul: He leadeth me in the (4)
    paths of rightousness for His name's sake. (5)
Yea, though I walk through the valley of the (6)
    shadow of death, I will fear no evil; for Thou (7)
    art with me; Thy rod and Thy staff they (8)
    comfort me. (9)
Thou preparest a table before me in the (10)
    presence of mine enemies; Thou anointest my (11)
    head with oil; my cup runneth over. (12)
Surely goodness and mercy shall follow me all (13)
    the days of my life: and I will dwell in the (14)
    house of the Lord forever. (15)

Here our initial attempt to reassign the symbol 'q' the new name pronounced 'shee' and the new unique task 'sh' was ultimately abandoned. Words like 'qephird' and 'qirlee' were so startling at first sight that we were immediately tempted to go back to the familiar convention for representing this sound. This feeling never waned, and we finally gave in to it. This was the *only* task assigned to 'q' so to do so meant dropping 'q', at admittedly little cost. Then the question arose about 'c' now named 'chee' with the unique task 'ch'. The problem is that we can't reasonably represent this sound with any traditional compound except 'ch' which inextricably involves 'c'. So 'c' would illogically appear always with a unique task but always in combination. In my own reaction, this change is much easier to swallow so we decided to just get used to it.

Sec V.2: Great Classic Poetry -- Old and New.

We can naturally expect that the *sound* of poetry will be adequately rendered by the new Modular English, as nearly phonic as it is and is designed to be. It is interesting nonetheless to sample over 600 years of English poetry to see how it *looks*, and what problems it might uncover.

We find the anonymous 14th century couplet written first in the Modular English Language and then in traditional Old English.

Epigram on thuh Yeer 1390-1

Thuh ax wuz sharp, thuh stok wuz hard,
In thuh xiii yeer uv King Ricard.

Compare Traditional Old English:

Epigram on the Yere 1390-1

The ax was sharpe, the stokke was harde,

In the xiii year of King Richard.

There's not a dime's worth of difference. It is reassuring to find that the English language has changed before, so hopefully we can find the will and the way to change it again.

An excerpt from Chaucer indicates that Olde English spelling and confusion of dialects were much the vogue before 1400. From his *Troilus and Criseyde*

And for ther is so gret diversite
In Englissh and in writyng of oure tonge,
So prey I God that non myswrite the,
Ne the mysmetre for defaute of tonge.

which we write in Modular English as

And for ther is soe graet dievirsitee
In Inglish and in wrieting uv owr tung,
Soe prae Ie God that nun misriet thee,
Nor thee mismeetir for deefolt uv tung.

Compare a contemporary English version:

And since there is such great diversity
In English and in writing of our tongue,
So I prey God that none miswrite thee,
Nor thy meter, for default of tongue.

Here 'God' is 'God' and not 'Gawd' because 'pot' and 'pod' define the soft 'o'. Similarly, 'default' becomes 'deefolt'. In both cases we ignore any possible subtle extension of the 'o' sound.

Our third example of classic poetry rendered in Modular Language, is said to have been written by Queen Elizabeth I around 1585. The first verse in Modular English becomes:

Wen Ie was Fer and Yung

Wen Ie wuz fer and yung, and faevir graesd mee,
Uv menee wuz Ie sot, ther mistres for too bee;
But Ie did skorn them ol, and ansird them therfor,
"Goe, goe, goe, seek sum uthirwer,
Importuen mee noe mor!"

Compare in Traditional English:

When I was Fair and Young

When I was fair and young, and favor graced me,
Of many was I sought, their mistress for to be;
But I did scorn them all, and answered them therefore,
"Go, go, go, seek some otherwhere,
Importune me no more!"

Here the translation of 'to' to 'too' has been used for emphasis. In ordinary prose 'to' might be elided to 'tuh' as in 'goeing tuh town'; but probably not here or in Shakespeare's 'too bee or not too bee'

This example likewise poses no difficulties to Modular English. Two things are quite clear. The first is that Modular English is completely capable of reproducing the sounds and rhythms of classic poetry.

There is a second lesson we should keep in mind: our contemporary English version of these early classics is already a much diluted version of the originals. It is an exercise in difficult scholarship to make sense, much less poetry, of the original manuscript of *Boewulf*. In fact every version read in English literature classes today is clearly labeled a translation.

We emphasize this point — perhaps more than we need to -- because a knee-jerk response to every proposal to reform the English language is the objection that we are 'abandoning our cultural heritage'. We are abandoning a damn-fool way of spelling and nothing more. As for *our* cultural heritage -- *whose* cultural heritage? Certainly not that of the 95+% of the world's people who *need* to know English as a second language in order to participate fully in world's scientific and commercial progress. As for the other 5% -- living in the USA and such numerically negligible enclaves as the former Great Britain – who speak, read, and write English as a first (and usually only) language, a large fraction of them need more help than they are currently getting to even access their cultural heritage in any written form.

As a final example of Modular English in classic modern poetry we vault across more than 3 centuries to Stephen Spender's uniquely *a propos* 1939 poem:

An Elementree Skool Klasroom in a Slum

Far far frum gustee waevz theez cildrenz faesez (1)
Liek rootles weedz, thuh her torn rownd ther palir. (2)
Thuh tol girl with hir waed-down hed. Thuh paepir- (3)
seeming boy, with rats eiz. Thuh stuntid, unlukee er (4)
Uv twistid boenz, reesieting a fotherz narld dizeez, (5)
Hiz lesin frum hiz desk. .... (6)
.... And yet, for theez (12)
Cildren, theez windoez, not this wirld, ar wirld, (13)
Wer ol ther fuecirz paentid with a fog, (14)
A neroe street seeld in with led skie, (15)
Far far frum riverz, caeps, and starz of wirdz. (16)
....
Unles, guvirnir, teecir, inspektir, visitir, (25)
This map bekumz ther windoe and theez windoez (26)
That shut upon ther lievz liek katakoemz, (27)
Braek Oe braek oepin til thae braek thuh town (28)
And shoe thuh cildren tuh green feeldz,
and maek ther wirld (29)
Run azhir on Goeld sandz, and let ther tungs (30)
Run naekid intuh books,
thuh wiet and green leevz oepin (31)
Historee therz hooz langwij is thuh sun. (32)

We bypass comparing to the original, confident that the reader has already mastered the simple rules of the new Modular English. It is interesting to compare the sociology of 1939 with that of the present. There is no identification of slums and poverty and limited lives with race or ethnicity. Nor is their any aspersion cast on the learning ability of the slum children. What does come through in Spender's poem is that these children in deep poverty are under such stress that they cannot spend the time and energy, or summon the concentration, to share fully in an education that takes them far afield from simple sustenance.

In this example we have elided 'to' into 'tuh' rather than use the more formal 'too', but not 'oepin' into 'oepn'. Both are possibilities depending on emphasis intended. 'Stuntid', 'twistid', 'paentid', and 'naekid' are rendered colloquially, 'narld' is elided as in the original spoken 'gnarled'. A new problem cropped up in our original scheme in 'azure' currently pronounced 'azh-ir'. It surely could not be represented with the 'sh' equivalent 'q' in place of 'z', nor was it common enough to merit it's own symbol. We have now eliminated that problem by abolishing 'q' altogether and retaining the soft 'sh' and the perfectly parallel hard 'zh'. The much reduced 'azhir' completely hits the mark of course, pending the inevitable 'azhr'.

Sec V.3: Shakesperian Drama.

Shakespeare is credited with being father to modern English. Many words were either coined by him or at least appeared in print first in his work. As we see in the accompanying list, a disproportionate number of these have ambiguous and non-euphonic spelling which will be changed rather radically in Modular English. Thus:

Shakespeare	translated to	**Modular English**
accommodation	becomes	akomadaeshn
assassination	becomes	asasinaeshn
dexterously	becomes	dextruslee
dislocate	becomes	disloekaet
indistinguishable	becomes	indistingwishabl
obscene	becomes	obseen
pedant	becomes	pedint

79

premeditated	becomes	preemeditaetd
reliance	becomes	reelieunts
submerged	becomes	submirjd.

There obviously are quibbles to be made: leave 'pedant' unchanged and agreeing with 'pedantik'. Agreed.

Shakespeare invented not only words but also phrases which -- although much used for 400 years -- have retained a certain piquancy that keeps them from ever becoming cliched. From *Hamlet* alone we retain:

> Too bee or not too bee: that iz thuh kwescun
> Mor in soroe than angir
> Brevitee iz thuh soel uv wit
> Thuh plaez thuh thing
> Fraeiltee, thie naem is wuhman
> Sumthing iz rotn in thuh staet of Denmark

None of these is harmed in the least by translation to Modular English. This is surely a result of what Samuel Johnson called Shakespeare's very creation of ''the diction of common life'', which underlies Modular English defined as it is -- and should be – by fundamental elementary English words.

We are confident that any and all of Shakespeare's art will survive translation into Modular Language. A good reason for this confidence is that Shakespeare's plays were meant to be *heard* so -- of course -- they are changed not atall by the translation. A final example from **Richard II** is doubly apropriate:

> Thuh langwij Ie hav lirnd thees fortee yeerz,
> Mie naetiv Inglish, now Ie must forgoe;
> And now mie tungz ues iz too mee noe mor
> Than an unstringd vieil or harp;
> Or liek uh kuning instruhment caesd up
> Or, beeing oepn, puht intoo hiz handz
> That noes noe tuc too tuen thuh harminee.

compare:

> The language I have learnt these forty years,
> My native English, now I must forego;
> And now my tongue's use is to me no more
> Than an unstringed viol or harp;
> Or like a cunning instrument cas'd up
> Or, being open, put into his hands
> That knows no touch to tune the harmony.

In fact, neither Richard's nor anyone else's power of speech will be impacted one iota by the conversion to Modular English. All the familiar words and phrases, all the subtle inflections and powerful emphases, all the grammatical niceties, ALL are still there. The only thing that has changed is the cock-a-mamie spelling conventions. And surely Richard and every other 40+ year old can make that change overnight in the interests of All Little Children, present and future.

Sec V.4: Prose -- Old and New.

Poetry and Drama are spoken art forms, and the impact on them of Modular English -- although visually jarring in their written form -- is not damaging. What do we find in Prose -- especially fiction -- where the written word is the artist's only contact with the audience. It seems a characteristic of great writers that they use a simple vocabulary and simple constructions.

We expect *Alice in Wonderland* to be readily accessible to bright 10 year old girls even 140 years after it was written, and even though it was written by a mathematician, hopefully a very singular one. In fact it is, and boring in any version of English. So let's look at Philip Roth's *The Conversion of the Jews* (1959) a children's story written for adults, and one of the funniest characterizations of teen-age boys ever. To set the stage: Ozzie has been pestering the Rabbi about whether or not -- if God can do Anything, as claimed -- the Mother of Jesus *could* in fact have been a virgin. In the ensuing outrage, Ozzie has fled to the

81

roof of the synagogue and the Fire Department has been summoned. Lets join them:

Thuh Konverzhun uv thuh Jooz

....
''Ozee, pleez kum down now.''

''Promis mee, promis mee ue'l nevir hit eneebudee abowt God.''

Hee had askt oenlee hiz muthir, but for sum reezn evreewun neeling in thuh street promisd hee wuhd nevir hit eneebudee abowt God.

Wunts agen ther wuz sielents.

''Ie kan kum down now, Muma,'' the boy on the roof fienlee sed. Hee tirnd hiz hed boeth waez az thoe ceking thuh trafik liets. ''Now Ie kan kum down.''

And hee did, riet intuh thuh sentir uv thuh yeloe net that gloed in thuh eevningz ej liek an oevirgroen haeloe.
......

Well, that wasn't so hard was it.

Everyone is writing like Hemingway, with a sixth grade vocabulary that poses no problems of spelling or multisyllabic words. So we turn to something completely foreign and necessarily in translation: Yukio Mishima's 1966 tragic tale *Patriotism*, chosen mainly for its more demanding vocabulary:

Paetryotizm

.... Lootenant Shinji Takaeyama uv thuh Koenoe Transport Batalyon -- proefowndlee distirbd bie thuh nolej that hiz kloesist koleegs had been muetineerz frum thuh beegining, and indignunt at thuh iminunt prospekt uv Impeeryul troops ataking Impeeryul troops -- tuhk hiz ofisirz sord and serimoenyulee disembowld himself in thuh frunt room uv hiz prievit rezidents in thuh 6th blok uv Aeoeba-coe, in Yotsooya Word. Hiz wief, Riekoe, foloed him, stabing hirself tuh deth. The lootenants ferwel noet konsistd uv wun sentents: "Long liv thuh Impeeryul Forsez." Hiz wiefs, aftir apolojeez for hir unfilyul kondukt in thus preeseeding hir parints tuh thuh graev, konkloodd: "Thuh dae wic, for a soljerz wief, had tuh kum, haz kum ......" Thuh last moements uv this heeroeik and dedikaetd kupl wir suc az tuh maek thuh godz themselvz weep. Thuh lootenants aej, it shuhd bee noeted, wuz 31, hiz wiefs 23; and it wuz not haf a yeer sints thuh selebraeshn uv ther merij.

It is a depressing but beautiful story. And it took an unusual amount of effort to translate it from the standard English translation of the original Japanese. The rendering of 'Patriotism' as 'Paetryotizm', and also 'Imperial' as 'Impeeryul', is obviously a compromise with some elision; similarly we took 'filial' to be 'filyul'; and 'ceremonially' to be 'serimoenyulee', which looks unwieldy but is only one letter longer. We have also opted for the informal 'tuh' which could easily be 'too' in places; also the informal 'thuh'. We have chosen 'disturbd', 'konsistd' and 'dedikaetd' for the past tense; and for consistency the unsightly 'konkloodd' and not 'konkloodd*ed*'. This was the most non-trivial translation we have faced so far. Interesting.

But having done it, what have we accomplished? Hopefully a beginning reader could read it with some hesitation on first try. Hopefully anyone could render the writing of it in a defensible version of Modular English. Words like 'patriot', 'imperial', 'ceremonially', 'filial', and also 'celebration' do give one momentary pause, as does 'concluded'.

Sec V.5: Lessons Learned.

We conclude on the basis of these few examples that Modular English is just as capable of faithfully expressing classic works of art as Standard English. In the spoken version of poetry and drama, there is intended to be no difference, and -- with the exception of a few elisions and a few personal choices of pronunciation -- we have achieved this at a high level of success.

There are visual impediments. The use of 'q' to represent the 'sh'-sound has been mentioned frequently as being shocking (as it is in 'qoking') and has ultimately been abandoned for the sake of a smoother transition to the new Modular English. The representation of the hard 'c' by 'k' gives everything a Germanic appearance which brings back memories of world wars and 'kommandants' not nearly as benevolent as commandos. Surely we will quickly get used to this minor visual impact and soon never notice it.

One of the restrictions we have imposed on Modular English is that the pronunciation should be achieved explicitly *without* decorating the individual letters with accent marks: so 'so' and 'sow' become 'soe' (except for pigs where 'sow' remains 'sow' and 'cow' becomes 'kow' as in 'how now brown kow').

Elided syllables are a problem that must be resolved by pronunciation: so 'even now' becomes 'eevn now'; 'evening' becomes 'eevning'; the poetic 'even-tide' might be emphasized to 'eeven-tied' or elided to 'eevn-tied' but not by decoration as in 'eev'n-tied'.

We have run into awkward situations in the past tense of verbs. Some like 'desired' as 'dezierd' (or eventually surely 'dzierd') and 'disturbed' as 'distirbd' are quite unequivocal. Others like 'consisted' are in the balance and can be rendered either way as 'konsistd' which is our preference, or 'konsistid' or 'konsisted'; but not 'konsist'd' or -- as in the example already given of a proposed modern phonics -- 'konsist.d'. There is another temptation especially difficult to resist as noted in the translation of 'concluded' as 'konkloodd' or even 'konklooded' which is also a possibility; but not by accent mark as in 'konklood'd'. To do so is to open the floodgates and drown all phonetic simplicity.

We are convinced that to relax the prohibition of accent marks would quickly undo all the good intentions of Modular English. Any and all decoration or subtlety or extreme abbreviation -- all these extra dimensions of complication -- must be eliminated to make the new Modular English accessible to All Little Children.

The benefit of making the change is obvious. All the nagging little spelling decisions about 'c' or 'k' or 'ck' or 'qu' are eliminated. This is not a problem for any of us, of course; but at what effort? Just hit 'Spell-Check' on your lap-top. At what cost? It's free! Long forgotten is the wasted time and effort that could have been spent in countless more enriching ways. And dare we think of the pain and suffering still being inflicted on those among us who can't remember, or who simply aren't interested in such inconsequential pursuits. Of course, they are *not* inconsequential, as everyone soon finds out. Remedial classes, second level education, your name forever on an education and career black-list. But worst of all is the ingrained and permanent feeling of failure; all because of a gratuitous, complicated, arbitrary, inconsistent, illogical spelling system. We behave like fraternity boys who have survived our own hazing ordeal and now seek to get even by inflicting the same degraded and degrading experience on others.

Next we turn to expository prose of the press, from politics, history, philosophy and from the sciences -- both social and anti-social. Here the writing is usually much less considerate of the reader, i.e. worse; the vocabulary more complicated; and the very purpose of writing is much different. How will Modular English fare at these diverse and demanding tasks?

CHAPTER SIX: MODULAR ENGLISH IN EXPOSITORY PROSE.

Sec VI.1: The Press.

Here we look at three groups contributing to newspapers: news, editorial, and sports columnists in a local newspaper (the Houston Chronicle) and a national one (the New York Times). The hectic pace of producing a daily paper precludes any in-depth editing or even any very deep reflection on the quality of the writing. Most of the local newspaper is devoted to lingerie ads and smarmy crime reports, the first of which requires no words, and neither of which requires any intellect. An example of the second -- which can be communicated equally well in any language, including Modular English -- is the following (authored by Deborah Tedford, Houston Chronicle, Mar 17, 2000, p.33A):

Man indietd for impirsunaeting law ofisir

A Huestin man hoo alejidlee intirveend in polees investigaeshnz wiel maskiraeding az a US marshl haz been indietd bie a fediral grand jiree. .....

A sekund kownt carjez him with pozesing 2 semee-otamatik wepnz, a 12-gaej shotgun and 2 rieflz. Heris sed it wuz ileegl for Fordtran to pozes the wepnz beekuz hee had been konviktd uv a kriem that had a punishment exeeding 1 yeer in prizn. .....

There is no hesitation in reading this but there are still ambiguities in translation. For example, 'Marshal' is unambiguous as 'marshl' but could be 'marshal' or '-il' or '-uhl' (but the same as 'martial'). 'Automatic' as 'otamatik' follows the informal pronunciation. An inconsistency would then arise in 'otamoebeel' which is abbreviated to 'otoe'; fortunately this word can usefully be dropped as needlessly pretentious in favor of 'kar' and 'truk', and as logically ambiguous anyway because it should include 'moetrsieklz'. More reverberations! Should it be 'biesiklz' or 'biesieklz'? Certainly we go 'siekling' not 'sikling' and better we should do it on our 'biesiekl'; and maybe best of all on our 'biek'.

We have opted for the shortest rendering of the elided '-ed' in the past tense of the verb 'intervened' as 'intirveend', which we consider unequivocal where there is no syllable; but also in 'indicted' as 'indietd', 'convicted' as 'konviktd' which we find sufficient and unambiguous even where there is a weak elided syllable. We still have the problem already mentioned of words like 'concluded' but we are inclined more and more to live with the '-dd' construction in 'konkloodd' for the sake of consistency. The only objection to it in the first place was aesthetic, and this barrier disappears with increasing familiarity.

Somewhat more important issues in somewhat more demanding prose appear in columns on the editorial page. Here is one replete with foreign names and places (by Daniel Benjamin and Steven Simon, Houston Chronicle Mar 17, 2000 p.41A)

Its in Indyaz handz tuh avirt disastr in Kashmeer

Olthoe Prezident Klintnz disizhn tuh vizit Pakistan haz reseevd mor atenshn, thuh moest important owrz uv hiz Azhuh trip wil bee spent toking with Indyaz leedirz. Sowth Azhuh iz kuhreening tuhword a kriesis, and it mae bee that oenlee an Indyan inishitiv kan avirt dizastr.

2 develipments ar haesning thuh kriesis; thuh ditiryoraeting reelaeshnship beetween Indya and Pakistan; and Pakistanz axeliraeting disintigraeshn. Boeth kuntreez hav testd nooklyir wepinz, and last sumir Pakistan-bakd militunts krosd intuh thuh Indyan-held Kargil reejn uv Kashmeer, neerlee sparking a ful-flejd wor. .....

Whew! Many problems! 'Disizhn' not 'deesizhn' because it's 'disied' not 'deesied' or even 'desied' as in 'deep' and 'det'. At least that's the way I speak. The elided ending '-izhn' replacing '-ision' seems unambiguous here. The hard 'zh' sound in 'Asia' has been easy as 'Azhuh'. A more explicit emphasis has been chosen for 'Indya' and 'Indyan'z'. Alternatives might be 'Inja' or 'Injya' but we prefer not. We have chosen 'haest' and 'haesn' but not 'haestn' according to common speech.

'Deteriorating' is a potential disaster as 'deeteer-eeoraeting'. We avoid this ludicrously painful precision for the more congenial elided version leading to 'ditiryoraeting'. This form is actually used to explain the pronunciation in my Thorndike-Barnhart Dictionary of 1952.

There are also quibbles over 'disintigraeshn', 'nooklyir' and 'militunt'.

An on-going quarrel threatens over dropping explicit vowels from elided endings as in the verb past tenses. This quarrel also occurs over the replacement '-tion' and '-sion' pronounced '-shun' but elided in ambiguous ways in informal speech to '-shin' to -- and this is the debate -- to '-shn'. A writer always has the option of indicating any particular emphasis by foregoing the fully elided ending and -- as in poetry -- enforcing the intended pronunciation. Our aim is to help All Little Children, and not to satisfy a pedantic self-proclaimed intelligentsia, so we go with '-shn'.

In fact, it seems that such foreshortening of the written language will inevitably take place once the floodgates of change are opened. Then who is to speak of correct? of right or wrong? The whole purpose of the written language -- as of the spoken language -- will be communication. The written word is a symbol intended to bring the word-thought to the mind of the reader. But simply being unambiguous is not sufficient, the symbol has also to be so familiar that we *immediately* have the intended thought in mind. We do not want to decipher a different encoding of it each time. For that reason, we must make the most radical changes in the first instance by anticipating common usage which will -- and should -- inevitably remove useless appendages such as silent vowels from the language. So we must have the courage to get rid of them from the start. In this way, we should choose the simplest and most economical symbol which unambiguously reminds us *as readers* of the spoken word. However, there is an over-riding primary concern: the spoken word *must* unambiguously remind us *as writers* of the symbol, that is of the spelling of the word. So what we want is one-to-one and reversible. It might be argued that we have that now, but at what cost! A rule for every occasion, and an exception to every rule.

Next we turn to the sports pages. Along with the stock market quotations, the sports section commands the most devoted audience. Who reads the sports pages? Middle-age, middle-income, middle-educated, non-athletic white guys who are in thrall to Michael Jordan and his successors; not teen-age athletes, many of whom neither know nor care who Michael Jordan was. Maybe the more accessible Modular English will nurture in all a love for reading not only the sports page but much more. From Dave Davidson's column in the Mar 26, 2000 *New York Times* SPORTS (p.35):

From the original:

McGwire doesn't understand that there is a
purpose: to globalize the game, something
Major League Baseball has been lax in doing.

Let the Japanese ..... see what real big-league
games are like ..... not just all-stars against
various Japanese teams in exhibition games that
don't count.

Translated into Modular English:

Muhgwier duznt undirstand that ther iz a
pirpuhs: tuh gloebaliez thuh gaem, sumthing
Maejr Leeg Baesbol haz been lax in dooing.

Let thuh Japaneez ..... see wut reel big-leeg
gaemz ar liek ..... not just ol-starz agenst
vereeus Japaneez teemz in exibishn gaemz that
doent kownt.

90

This was and remains quite trivial, but in fact is simpler in Modular English. Maybe 'exabishn' after the careless way we speak, rather than carrying along the connection to 'exhibit' pronounced -- and now spelled.-- 'exibit'. How is a third or fourth grade boy supposed to cope with words even as simple as 'purpose', 'globalize', 'league' and 'exhibition' on first sight? And yet the sports page should be devoured by every aspiring athlete just out of interest. It is *not,* for the very good reason that many little athletes can't read easily and don't like to be reminded of their shortcoming. It's a large part of the reason they seek a refuge in sports.

Sec VI.2: Philosophy.

No other subject puts the language under such extreme stress as the philosophy of science which seeks to answer the question "What is it that scientists are *really* doing?" in such general terms that the philosophers – who might not know or care about any particularity of science -- can remain safely aloof from the hurly-burly of the evolving knowledge which constitutes the daily reality of the practitioners of science. For this role of critic-analyst-censor, the ability of the philosophers to construct an impregnable logic, in clear and precise prose accessible to non-specialists, which encompasses *all* the various very specialized codes of science -- often mathematics of a very abstract sort -- is the *sine qua non* of participation. The world-view they construct transcends that of any particular individual science and seeks an understanding of the nature of knowledge itself as it is manifested in the most diverse of scientific endeavors. The question is: Can Modular English cope with the philosophy of science? Here is a brief excerpt from the section of the *Encyclopaedia Britannica* discussing the scope of the subject:

From the original:

..... The crucial question it poses is: "What is a concept?" ..... the Viennese Positivists had condemned any tendency to regard the philosophy of science as concerned with scientific thinking — which was ..... a matter for psychologists -- and had restricted themselves to the formal analysis of scientific arguments. ..... To interpret a concept such as force as ..... a feeling ..... or ..... a mental image could lead, they argued, only to confusion. ..... the concepts of science ..... were simply translated into logical or linguistic questions about formal roles and empirical references of ..... mathematical variables.

Translated into Modular English:

..... Thuh krooshl kwescn it poezz iz: "Wut iz a konsept?" ..... thuh Veeaneez Pozativists had kondemd enee tendensee tuh reegard thuh filosofee uv sieents az konsirnd with sieentifik thinking — wic wuz ..... a matir for siekolajists -- and had reestriktd themselvz tuh thuh forml analasis uv sieentifik arguements. ..... Tuh intirpret a konsept suc az fors az ..... a feeling ..... or ..... a mentl imaj kuhd leed, thae argued, oenlee tuh konfuezhn. ..... thuh konsepts uv sieents ..... wir simplee tranzlaetd intuh logikl or lingwistik kwescnz abowt forml roelz and empeerikl refirensz uv ..... mathmatikl vereeablz.

There is no new problem in communicating the intent of the prose in the translation. It is every bit as clear as it was in the original traditional English. Some now familiar constructions reappear: 'poses' as 'poezz' for example. We have noticed a common problem for the first time: we miss the '-c-' as '-ts-' in 'tendency' and 'references' and have resolved the ugliness of the '-ts-' construction by eliding the sounds to 'tendensee' and 'referensz'. This must be a peculiarity of my own speech because -- once more -- my old dictionary comes to the rescue with just this '-s-' pronunciation prescribed for both words.

In any case, it is reassuring that Modular English handles this weighty assignment with such aplomb. Isn't 'kwescnz' a beautiful kick! Perilously close to 'bfstk' though.

Sec VI.3: Social Science.

From the Mar 21, 2000 NYT Science section we find a discussion by Jane E. Brody of Post-Traumatic Stress Disorder in young people, intended for a wide audience of above average literacy level. It will be our thesis that the failure experienced by many little children trying to master the mysteries and complexities of reading and spelling traditional English is a serious form of traumatic stress. Brody cites primarily more explosive sorts of causes -- often localized in a single violent event -- which do not directly relate to the gradual long term degrading experience of failure in elementary education. It is our view that the virtual confinement of the child in -- for some – a hostile environment without hope, and without end, constitutes traumatic stress by an unintended but nonetheless real emotional abuse.

From the original:

... The disorder is characterized by three main symptom complexes that can be socially and emotionally crippling ..... and interfere with learning. The symptoms ..... [include] irritability, outbursts of anger, difficulty concentrating or completing tasks. ..... among children, the most frequent causes of PTSD ..... [include] emotional abuse by parents or others involved in providing care ..... the risk of developing the disorder ..... in children ..... more than half ... the avoidance behavior may result in lost experiences important for success throughout life. .....

Translated into Modular English:

..... Thuh disordir iz karaktiriezd bie 3 maen simtum komplexz that kan bee soeshalee and imoeshnlee kripling ..... and intirfeer with lirning. Thuh simtums ..... [inklood] eeritabilitee, owtbirsts of angir, difikultee konsentraeting or kompleeting tasks. .... amung cildren, thuh moest freekwunt kozz uv PTSD ..... [inklood] imoeshnl abues bie perents or uthirs involvd in provieding ker ..... thuh risk uv diveleping thuh disordir ..... in cildren ..... mor than haf ..... thuh avoyduns beehaevyir mae reezult in lost expeeryunsz important for suxes thruhowt lief. ....

The translation of 'throughout' as 'thruhowt' is almost as awful as the original. One avoids the too strict 'throo-owt' with 'throo' as in 'spool' because it's ugly even with the hyphen and intolerable without it; and wishes for 'thruowt' but the unadorned 'u' has been committed to the 'but' sound; 'thrueowt' is neither true nor possible to pronounce; we have settled on the much elided 'thruhowt' as in 'puht' for 'put' and 'buhk' for 'book'; 'threw' has been eliminated in favor of 'throo' which returns us to the ugliness above. For the moment, we choose 'thruhowt' over 'throo-owt'.

Other translation difficulties are familiar: 'complexes' as 'komplexz' gives one a bit of a start, but the '-xz' plural is quite logical and sufficient. The similar results for 'causes' as 'kozz' and 'experiences' as 'expeeryunsz' also take some getting used to, but only until we remind ourselves that there are NO silent letters: each letter has a separate job to do.

We must keep in mind also that the job is not unique, as illustrated by the cases of 'e' (with three jobs as in 'pet' and 'deer' and enforcing hard vowel sounds in 'raet' for 'rate'), 'h' (also three as in 'hat', 'with', and 'puht' for 'put'), 'o' (with three as in 'dot', 'pool', and the hard sound as in 'boet' for 'boat'), and 'u' (again three as in 'but', 'muel' for 'mule' and again 'puht' for 'put'). The vowels 'a' and 'i' are soft unless forced to be hard by an immediately following 'e'. The hard consonants have unique jobs with the sole exception of the 't' forced by the accompanying 'h' to be as in 'with'. Soft consonants like 'h', 'w' and 'y' have special 'modifying' tasks illustrated by 'hi' and 'high' now as 'hie', 'why' now as 'wie' and 'yodel' now as 'yoedl'. Hard consonants with new assignments are 'c' as 'ch' as in 'suc' for 'such'. Earlier attempts to use 'q' for 'sh' as in 'qirlee' for 'surely' have been abandoned and 'surely' becomes 'shirlee'; the hard 'zh' sound is made explicit as in 'decision' which becomes 'disizhn'. The letter 'q' is no longer used.

PTSD is described for professionals in the *American Psychiatric Association* Diagnostic Manual of Mental Disorders (4th Edition, p.426):

In traditional English:

..... Frequently, the disturbance initially meets criteria for Acute Stress Disorder in the immediate aftermath of the trauma. The symptoms of the disorder and the relative predominance of reexperiencing, avoidance, and hyperarousal symptoms may vary over time. ..... The severity, duration, and proximity of an individual's exposure to the traumatic event are the most important factors ..... In PTSD, the stressor must be of an extreme (i.e., life-threatening) nature. In contrast, in Adjustment Disorder, the stressor can be of any severity. .....

As translated into Modular English:

..... Freekwuntlee, thuh distirbants inishulee meets krieteerya for Akuet Stres Disordir in thuh imeedyut aftirmath uv thuh troma. Thuh simtumz uv thuh disordir and thuh relativ pridominunts uv reexpeeryunsing, avoydunts, and hiepirarowzl simtumz mae veree oevr tiem. ..... Thuh severitee, diraeshn, and proximitee uv an indivijoolz xpoezhr tuh thuh tromatik event ar thuh moest importnt faktirs ..... In PTSD, thuh stresir must be uv an xtreem (i.e., lief-thretning) naecr. In kontrast, in Ajustment Disordir, the stresir kan bee uv enee severitee. .....

The professional vocabulary uncovers some new translation experiences. The rendering of 're-ex-per-i-enc-ing' as ''ree-x-peer-yuns-ing' looks cumbersome but in fact introduces only one more letter. The syllabic split of the word is changed as shown and makes use of the usual elision into '-yuns-'. 'Hyperarousal' would benefit from hyphenation in either version of English, but is completely unequivocal in Modular English as 'hiepirarowzl'. Other translations such as 'duration' as 'diraeshn', 'individuals' as 'indivijoolz', 'exposure' as 'xpoezhr', 'extreme' as 'xtreem' and 'nature' as 'nacr' are quite a revelation of just how radical the change can be.

We will have more to say about the professionals' restriction of PTSD to the result of isolated physically events. We view this as too restrictive and will extend the definition to include the ego-damage and the *permanent* loss of self-esteem suffered by little children disheartened by repeated failure to master the arcana of traditional written English.

Although the translation of the full-fledged professional psychiatric text to Modular English was a bit of a revelation in places, it was straightforward and resulted in a text with the full meaning intact. We can ask no more of the new Modular English. The strange appearance of some individual words can best be judged only after some experience with Modular English, keeping in mind the new permissive philosophy that the written language must always be a matter of judgement and remain a work in progress. Samuel Johnson knew this and people have constantly preached it but they really believed that the language should change somehow *only* at the edges. Now we require that the written language have only a few immutable factors -- the small set of fundamental monosyllabic words which define the tasks of the letters of the alphabet -- and *nothing else* is carved immutably in stone, *everything* else becomes a matter of judgement. Some of these judgements are easy and seem essentially unique. One of these illustrates the problem: 'becomes' becomes 'beekumz'. Or does it? Some people sometimes say 'bikumz', or more rarely 'bekumz' with 'bek-' as in 'bed'; almost inevitably we end up eliding to 'bkumz'. What has been lost? Certainly not argumentation. What has been gained, however, goes far beyond this simple word. What has been gained is the trust of All Little Children in the ability of their elementary skills and judgements to take them everywhere.

Sec VI.4: Physical Science.

Scientific journals are notorious for bad writing, arcane and specialized vocabularies and -- most unforgivable of all -- the use of acronyms, all without providing a glossary, thus guaranteeing that nobody can understand the reports without an extensive background. It is difficult to imagine that much harm could be suffered by their questionable comprehensibility from a change in spelling conventions. We look at three lower levels of scientific communication intended for less specialized readers and written with greater attention to readability: first from a column in the *New York Times* Science Section; then an excerpt from an introductory physics text; and finally an excerpt from an advanced text.

James Glanz in the Feb 1, 2000 NYT Science Section writes in a column "Theory, Reality and Skeptical Tourists in Physics Land" about the gulf between scientists and the philosophers who seek to identify, evaluate and assimilate the gist of scientific theorizing:

.... In fakt, in thuh speerit uv filosofikl empeerasizm, theereez get reeviezd in liet uv fresh evidents thae kanot explaen. Sumtiemz thuh need for laetir reevizhn iz kleer evn az thuh theereez ar beeing diviezd: neerlee ol modirn theereez uv matir and enirjee ar kold "efektiv feeld theereez". Az Dr. Fulir's buhk reekownts ..... "Thu reezn wun theeree beekumz dominant iz beekuz uv loekalee spesifik, soeshl faktirz wic then get a kiend uv institueshnl moementum at wun tiem," Dr. Fulir sed uv hiz oen vuez, wic doo alow for a konekshn beetween fizix and reealitee. Thuh distants beetween thuh 2 vuez iz soe graet that klishae-maekirz hav koynd thuh tirm "sieents worz" to deskrieb ther intirakshn.

Only a few small quibbles surface in this example. 'Filosofikl' could more phonetically require 'fili-' or 'fila-' according to elided speech, but we retain the connection to 'filosofir'. The ending '-ikl' is sufficient and in accord with our developing conviction -- which could most sensibly evolve to become a general principle -- to shorten wherever possible by dropping such unnecessary and ambiguous vowels. 'Devised' becomes 'diviezd' in accord with our well-worn old dictionary. We have for the sake of consistency rendered all '-shun-' sounds by 'shn' as in 'institueshnl', 'konekshn' and 'intirakshn'. Only a residual timidity restrains us from 'institooshnl'. Rooty toot toot, three cheers for the institoot. 'Kli-' not 'klee-' in 'cliché'.

In his admirable introductory physics text, Eugene Hecht writes on Newton's Laws:

> Iezik Nuetn set owt thuh "axeeumz or loz uv moeshn" ..... *"Evree bodee kontinuez in a staet uv rest or uv ueniform moeshn in a straet lien exept insoefar az it iz kompeld too caenj that staet bie forsez impresd upon it"* .....
>
> A nue ekwivalents is dron heer beetween rest and Ueniform moeshn. Oltiring eethir reekwierz a fors, but wunts eethir staet iz establishd, it pirsists forevir in thuh absents uv fors. .....
>
> Nuetn felt that *inirsha* -- that iz, *thuh rezistunts too a caenj in moeshn* -- woz an intrinzik propirtee uv matir itself, independent uv thuh enviernment.
>
> ..... fizisists hav sirtnlee not yet reezolvd thuh fundamentl kwescn uv thuh orijin uv inirsha. ....

Here 'laws' and 'paws' (and 'pause') become 'loz' and 'poz' because 'law' and 'paw' have the fundamental 'lot' and 'pot' vowel sound. This leaves us with 'loyirz' praktising 'lo' in their 'lo praktis' -- again a marvelous coincidence! 'Praktis' is the pronunciation given in my old dictionary. Note the economy of 'certainly' as 'sirtnlee'. We considered leaving 'fundamental' unchanged, resisting the '-ntl' temptation. However this change became irresistible when we considered also the pressure from '-mental' as '-mentl' in 'jujmentl', 'departmentl', 'elementl' etc, etc. We enforce the American 'eethir' over the British 'iethir', but would readily accept 'eethr' as well. What about the Standard English 'ether'? It also becomes 'eethr' with the soft 'th' but is distinguished only by the context, which is solely the responsibility of the author.

In his definitive text *The Quantum Theory of Fields*, Steven Weinberg addresses the same subject as Glanz above. Here we provide the original and the translation because the discussion is somewhat technical.

The original:

Although non-renormalizable theories can provide useful expansions in powers of energy, they inevitably lose all predictive power at energies of the order of the common mass scale M which characterizes the various couplings. If we were to take these expansions literally, the results for S-matrix elements would violate unitarity bounds for energies much greater than M.

and the translation to Modular English:

Olthoe non-reenormaliezabl theereez kan provied uesfuhl expanshnz in powirz uv enirjee, thae inevitablee looz ol prediktiv powir at enirjeez uv thuh ordir uv thuh komon mas skael M wic keraktiriezez thuh veryus kuplingz. If wee wir tuh taek theez expanshnz litiralee, the reezults for S-maetrix elements wuhd vielaet ueniteritee bowndz for enerjeez muc graetir than M.

In making the translation of this excerpt, many of the questions were already resolved by previous experience. It would have been natural in physics to give greater emphasis to 'expansions' but our decision that '-sion' and '-tion' 'shun' sounds be rendered '-shn' had already been made, so 'expansions' becomes 'expanshnz'. We have waffled over 'characterizes' as 'karaktiriezez', which reminds us of the similar problem with 'concluded' which was resolved as 'konkloodd'. We might still swallow hard and go for 'karakteriezz' on the principle that there are NO silent letters, so '-zz' MUST be pronounced, here as '-iezez'. 'Literally' has been rendered 'litiralee' but it seems inevitable that it is really headed for the maximally elided form 'litrlee'.

Sec VI.5: Lessons Learned.

It was here in the first development of Modular English that the decision was taken after much agonizing to make a major compromise and retain the traditional representation of the explicit '-sh-' sound as '-sh-' rather than compactifying it into a new job for 'q'. The pressure to do so became overwhelming from a number of sources. First, the appearance of many common words became quite bizarre, strange and awkward. Examples abound, but 'she' as 'qe', 'decision' as 'deesiqn' and many more too numerous to recount, were a constant irritant. Second, it was apparent that this radical change in the appearance of the written language would be a serious deterrent to its acceptance. Third, the hard '-zh-' sound in 'vision' must be distinguished from the soft '-sh-' sound in 'mission, just as the hard 'z' at the end of 'seize' (and 'sees' and 'seas') as 'seez' must be distinguished from the soft 's' at the beginning of these same words. This is nicely done with the traditional 'sh' and 'zh', and we were finally forced here to admit that compound expressions of these sounds should be granted the same legitimacy as that given to 'th'. Our effort to reassign the 'sh' task to 'q' was therefore abandoned here and eliminated from the start; leaving no task for the letter 'q' which has therefore been dropped from the alphabet. We have never felt the same pressure to distinguish a hard 'th' as in the distinction between 'with' and 'the'.

This important compromise in the principle of economy of expression will contribute much to the ease with which those already literate make the transition to the new Modular English.

The ultimate result of our brief sample of readings from these diverse sources -- literature, both prose and poetry; the press; philosophy; social science; and physical science – shows explicitly that Modular English is fully capable of performing _**ALL**_ the tasks done by traditional English.

The compelling need to make the tremendous upheaval involved in the change cannot be overemphasized. We are wasting tremendous human and material resources in a losing battle to impose the archaic structure of the traditional English written language. The competition for the minds, the time, and the attention of All Little Children is being irrevocably lost to the competing forces of our modern world.

Some of these forces have no redeeming social value -- here we can list video and computer games, and the popular media including TV and movies -- but they combine in a gigantic industry which is economically powerful and compellingly seductive and designed solely to exploit immature children and young adults. Our society has no will to curb their destructive influence on our children, and these destructive industries have no more reason to moderate their own lucrative trade than do their street cousins the drug-pushers. It seems that we must learn to function in an environment saturated by their siren call.

Other forces are quite the opposite. The proliferation of knowledge is exponential. The demands put on students today are far greater in breadth if not in depth than anything ever confronted before in history. Time is spent in grade school studying computers, sociology, psychology, and other subjects we had never imagined. Genetics, micro-biology, and much that is new and mysterious in the traditional sciences of biology, chemistry and physics. There is an accelerated pace in mathematics, greater emphasis on foreign languages, a complexity and immediacy of the world and its people and its problems.

We simply cannot continue to demand that All Little Children make the same investment in mastering the complexities of a language that is needlessly chaotic and complex. If we can make it simpler -- and we not only can but here we have -- *then we **MUST***.

CHAPTER SEVEN: MODULAR ENGLISH: UNIQUE? NOT EXACTLY.

Sec VII.1: Looking for Trouble and Finding It.

The goal in this chapter is to play the devil's advocate to see how unique -- or at worst how recognizable -- the Modular English spelling is for a cross-section of words chosen more or less at random, by picking one word from every tenth page of my old and admittedly trivial desk dictionary. We have to be prepared for a considerable lack of uniqueness. It is essential to keep in mind the new attitude toward spelling embodied in Modular English. Written Modular English is no longer the class-room bully, it does not have the responsibility of censor or even disciplinarian, or of being the language policeman to the world's English language speakers, nor is it the defender of some ancient culture, nor is it the window through which we view a classic literature unchanged. Modular English expressly renounces every such mixed agenda for one purpose and one purpose alone. That purpose is to make spelling, writing and reading easier for All Little Children.

The way we seek to do this is to have the written word correspond to the spoken word. To the extent that a person succeeds in putting in print an unmistakably intelligible symbol of his spoken intent, that person has succeeded in spelling. That does not mean that every idiosyncratic rendering of a word is defendable. Communication is the goal, and the literate reader is the ultimate judge. What it does mean is that there is successful and unsuccessful spelling. There is also correct and incorrect spelling. The difference in Modular English is that there is a continuum between correct and incorrect. Unsuccessful spelling is always incorrect. Successful spelling can range from fully correct -- if it succeeds in communicating the writer's intent most easily for the reader; partially correct if the reader has to struggle with an awkward or unfamiliar construction which can be improved; and incorrect if the reader is misled or unable after a modest effort to decipher the writer's attempt.

Because the written language is patterned after and subservient to the spoken language, accent and emphasis can change spelling. This usually results when excessively formal, self-conscious or pretentious enunciation is employed; so for example 'accentuate' can run the gamut from the very formal and precise 'axsentueaet' to the maximally elided -- and here preferred -- 'axencuhaet' where we remind that 'c' is 'chee' with the sole task of representing the 'ch' sound, and 'uh' is as in 'put' now written 'puht'. This last is in fact once again the recommended pronunciation in my old dictionary. Is it unique? By no means. 'Axencoowaet' does the job for people choosing to speak this way, or maybe sing this way in the old song ''Yuh gota axencoowaet thuh positiv, eeliminaet thuh negativ .....''.

Emphasis can also make explicit any vowels which are usually elided. For standard speech -- not necessarily representative of England, India, or many other English speakers with different accents and speech patterns -- we try as a guiding principle to maximize the elision and shorten the written word as much as possible while still having an unmistakable representation of the spoken intent.

Now we cruise through some 100 words to see what arguments, difficulties, ambiguities and absurdities crop up.

Sec VII.2: A Survey of the Dictionary.

abscissa -- absisa. The problem is how to represent the last syllable. A soft 'a', 'e' or 'u' would convey the word adequately. My first choice of 'a' coincides with the recommended pronunciation in my dictionary.

acquiesce -- akwiyes. This was remarkably easy and convincing. But the world will not akwiyes easily to Modular English.

advocasy -- advikasee. The '-oca-' syllable is the problem here. The dictionary recommends '-aca-'. We have followed our principle of maximum elision, and omit the 'o' but keep an 'i' in deference to the related verb 'advikaet' and noun 'advikat'.

Albequerque – Albakirkee, is quite compelling and agrees with the recommendation of my old dictionary.

altercation -- oltirkaeshn. We find this unambiguous, arguing from 'hot' to 'halt' as 'holt' to 'alt' as 'olt'.

anaemic -- aneemik.

antibiotic -- antibieotik, in agreement with the dictionary recommendation. 'Antee-' is also a possibility.

arrogance – eragans, again in agreement with the dictionary. '-ants' is also possible, depending on accent and emphasis.

appreciation -- apreeshiaeshn. Will be a long time coming for these efforts.

avaricious – avarishus is recommended. My first choice was 'avir-'.

atrocious -- atroeshas as recommended by my old dictionary.

bass – baes or bas depending on the intent.

balk -- bok along with 't/alk', 'w/alk', 'c/aulk', 'h/awk', 'sh/ock', and many others.

bibliophile -- bibliafiel is recommended by the dictionary. Various degrees of ugliness like 'bibleeoefiel' result from too strict elocution.

Belgium -- Beljum.

boloney or bologna – baloenee or even bloenee. 'Buhloenee' perhaps as a mild expletive.

blasphemy -- blasfumee. What many people consider tampering with God-given English to be.

brochure -- broeshr is unmistakable and preferred to the unelided '-ir'.

boycott -- boykot. One way 5,000,000 children could force schools to convert to Modular English.

calculation -- kalkyalaeshn appears ugly but unavoidable and unambiguous. The second syllable could be '-yul-' or '-yool-' but we prefer the softer '-yal-'.

capitulate -- kapicalaet. What school boards will be happy to do when they realize how much money they can save.

carriage -- kerij. At last, a compaction and precisely the dictionary recommended pronunciation.

cauterize -- kotiriez.

character -- keraktr. The unelided '-ir' ending has been avoided.

chlorophyll -- klorafil.

circumlocution -- sirkmloekueshn. Maximum elision of 'circum-' and '-tion'.

coach -- koec.

colloquial -- koloekwyal. We have resisted the hard syllable '-weel' for the softer two syllable '-wyal' recommended in the dictionary, but both do the job quite unambiguously.

commercialization -- komirshliezaeshn. Seven illogical constructions – six of them in a row -- are eliminated: '-c/i/al/i/za/tion'; and a long word made explicitly rational, with even a slight decrease in the length.

condescend -- kondisend is recommended, but 'kondesend' or 'kondeesend' are possible and unambiguous.

consign -- konsien. Whole libraries will be consigned to the recycling centers.

cooperate -- koeopraet or koeopiraet seem unavoidable. The unelided '-ir-' seems more natural in 'koeopiraeshn' but 'koeopraeshn' is unmistakable.

counterfeit -- kowntirfit or even 'kowntrfit'.

credential -- kridenshl is recommended. Only self-conscious enunciation could lead to 'kredenshul' or '-shal' or '-shil' or '-shel' or even '-shuhl'. The benefit of the principle of maximum elision is convincingly illustrated by this case and many like it.

culture -- kulcr. One for the Gipper.

daffodil -- dafadil is recommended and natural, although 'dafedil' is possible and acceptable.

decadence -- dekadans. A very expensive symptom of which is a written language by, for, and of the intelligentsia.

deceive -- deeseev. No probleme.

dementia -- dimenca is obvious and clear and recommended by my dictionary over the only other possible candidate 'demenca'.

destructible -- distruktabl. Any argument or ambiguity here is resolved by the rule -- *always* '-abl'.

difference -- difrens, again by maximum elision. Preferred over such challengers as 'difirents' or a closer contender 'difrent' and hence 'difrents'.

discourteous -- diskirtyus.

distraught -- distrot. God love All Little Children and make their lives easier.

doubtful -- dowtfal avoiding the too prissy '-fuhl'.

drudgery -- drujree. Eliminate the drudgery of old-fashioned spelling.

earthquake --irthkwaek.

effloresce -- eflores.

empirical -- empeerakl again, as in my old dictionary.

enough -- inuf is recommended over 'eenuf' or even 'enuf'.

erudition -- eryadishn.

eventful -- iventfl is recommended over '-fal' or '-fuhl', again cutting the Gordian knot by the principle of maximum elision, which is after all just anticipating the inevitable.

experimental -- experamentl or even 'expermentl'.

fallacious -- falaeshus.

felicitous -- falisatus.

finality -- fienalitee.

flaw -- flo also in 'jaw', 'law', 'saw', 'paw' and 'pa', all patterned after 'pot' without the 't'.

folklore -- foeklor.

fortunate -- forcanat.

frightful -- frietfuhl.

galaxy -- galaxee.

genealogy -- jeenyolajee, but variants are possible including 'jeniolajee'.

girl -- girl and 'boy' remains 'boy', fundandamental elements defining Modular English usage.

good English -- guhd Inglish. What our mothers taught us.

Great Britain -- Graet Britn.

guarantee -- gerantee.

half -- haf. Half the world's children -- all those speaking, wanting to speak, and needing to speak English will benefit immediately from the adoption of Modular English.

haughty -- hotee.

heir -- er. Also 'air' and 'err' become 'er', pronounced as in 'berry' and 'hairy' and 'vary' all as '-er/ee'.

highlight -- hieliet.

homonym -- homanim. Homonyms will have one spelling with the intended meaning determined by the context, as it already is in the spoken language.

Houston --Huestn.

hypochondriac -- hiepakondryak.

immeasurable -- imezhrabl.

inaccessible -- inaxesabl.

Indianapolis -- Indyanapilis.

influential -- influhencl in my old dictionary.

instinctive -- instinktiv. What spelling should, can, and will be with Modular English.

intractable -- intraktabl. What much of spelling is now for at least 1/3 of English speaking people even after a tremendous personal effort and a very expensive but unavailing investment by their school systems.

island – ielnd ideally but perhaps ieland is easier on old eyes.

jettison -- jetisn. Logical fate of ninety percent of the books -- never circulated in the last ten years -- in all the libraries.

juvenile -- joovniel is sufficient. More of whom will be happy and successful students with a full portion of self-esteem if we switch to Modular English and allow them to succeed in their studies.

knack -- nak of Modular English is very easy for everyone.

laissez faire -- lezae fer. The predominating principle of Modular English.

laughable -- lafabl.

lenient -- leenyant. Modular English is accused of being too (fill in the blank).

likelihood -- lieklihuhd.

litigous -- latijus or perhaps even ltijus, but no, that's too ugly.

loquacious -- loekwaeshas.

machination -- makanaeshn with only a minor question over 'maki-', also acceptable.

manageable -- manajabl eliminating two silent vowels and one ambiguous consonant. The '-abl' ending is universal and not to be tampered with.

marriage -- merij is recommended in my old dictionary.

measurable -- mezhrabl. The '-ir' in my old dictionary's pronunciation has fallen prey to the principle of maximum elision.

meretricious -- meratrishus, as in my old
THORNDIKE -- BARNHART *Comprehensive Desk Dictionary* published in 1952.

militia -- malisha avoiding the possible 'mlisha' only out of cowardice.

Mississippi -- Misasipa to the natives, Misasipee to the rest of us.

monosyllable -- monasilabl.

mountaineer -- mowntneer.

naivete -- naheevtae not easy! My pronunciation is 'nie/eev/e/tae'. My dictionary is unyielding on a breathy 'a' as in 'far' and a hard 'ev' which we enforce with the 'nah/eev/tae' but this is ambiguous as 'na/heev/tae'. A compromise might be an ordinary soft 'a' and 'na/eev/tae' but this is ambiguous as 'nae/evtae'. The only unambiguous rendition would seem to be my hard 'i', and the rest as in the dictionary giving 'nieeevtae' which is unsightly but the only resolution I have for the moment. After further consideration, I prefer 'nah/eev/tae' with the accent on the second syllable and we have to remember the 'a' goes with the 'h'.

negotiable -- negoeshabl.

noblesse oblige -- noebles oebleezh in my dictionary.

noticeable -- noetisabl. ALL '-able'/'-ible' ambiguities will be resolved once and for all and forever with '-abl'.

obeisance -- obaesens in my dictionary.

Odysseus -- Oedisoos on his Odisee.

opposition -- opazishn.

ostracize -- ostrasiez.

Pacific -- Pasifik.

panegyric -- panajeerik is recommended although I would have favored '-jierik'.

partiality -- parshialitee or 'parshyalitee' equally well.

peaceable -- peesabl. Something that the enforced transition to Modular English promises not to be.

perfectible -- pirfektabl. That which Modular English spelling has no pretensions to being. Perfection means absolutism. We are trying to define a rational written form of speech. Spoken English has dialect, accent, emphasis, all of which may be represented in differing ways within the *consistent* Modular English assignment of tasks to the various letters of the alphabet.

petroleum -- petroelyam. After recent gouging by OPEC, now half the price of bottled *pure spring* (yeah, really! we guarantee it) water.

physiognomy -- fizeeognamee or fizyognamee equally well.

plagiarize -- plaejiriez or even plaejriez.

pneumonia -- noomoenya or nuhmoenya.

population -- popyalaeshn over the harder popuelaeshn.

pragmatism -- pragmatizm. The overall ruling principle of Modular English.

prestige -- presteej.

profanation -- proefnaeshn using maximal elision, which communicates the speaker's intent perfectly well.

protege -- proetazhae.

pusillanimous – puesilanamus.

quarrelsome -- kworlsum. Characterizes all failed and ineffectual phoneticists who also have in common the fact that they (we?) are all late-middle aged, white and geeky.

quotient -- kwoeshant or even 'kwoeshnt'.

ration -- rashn. We seek to 'rashnliez' the spelling of English.

recuperate -- rekoopiraet.

reign, rein, rain -- raen.

reservoir -- rezavor.

reverential -- revirencl again applying the Occam's razor of the principle of maximum elision.

rite -- riet as are 'right' and 'write'.

Rosh Hashana -- Rosh Hashana although 'Roesh' is favored by some. It is interesting that so many words and place names are taken over into English with a near perfect phonetic spelling -- witness Tripoli, Madagascar, and Constantinople.

sacrilege -- sakralij.

sanctuary -- sangcuheri recommended by my dictionary, but this word is an unexpected challenge. Excessive enunciation could lead to 'sankcooeree' as in 'sank/coo/er/ee' with the ambiguous '-ooe-' structure. In this case the 'oo/e' resolution follows sequentially rather than the 'o/oe' which seems impossible to pronounce. A comparable triple vowel structure occurred in 'cooperate' as 'koe/opiraet' which was unsightly but unambiguous. Such awkward constructions seem to be symptomatic of overzealous enunciation and -- hopefully -- can be resolved by more vernacular pronunciations like the one above.

scrupulous -- skroopyalas is recommended by my dictionary. Not all words are going to be beautiful to see and we just have to accept this fact.

self-evident -- self-evident or less facetiously, '-evadant'. What Modular English spelling will be.

sequestration -- sikwestraeshn is recommended here, although my dictionary includes the 'see-' possibility.

should -- shuhd.

slaughter -- slotr or perhaps slotir for the insecure who feel safer with half-measures. Either is obvious, easy and a significant simplification.

solicitous -- solisitus according to my speech pattern, but 'solisatas' is recommended in my dictionary.

sovereignty -- sovrantee.

spiritualism -- speericalizm or perhaps 'speericuhlizm'. My dictionary renders the '-ual-' explicitly as two syllables, but this is needless.

statutory -- stacuhtoree as pronounced in my old dictionary, but easy on the '-ee'.

structural -- strukcirl although strukcrl is unambigous and just requires a bit more courage.

subtle -- sutl.

superior -- sapeeryir is recommended in my dictionary, but 'suh-' is included as an option.

syringe -- srinj. One more for the Gipper.

taut -- tot, as are 'taught' and 'tot'.

tenuous -- tenueus employs a hard 'ue' which is elided in my old dictionary, and might not survive common usage.

thesis -- theesis, plural 'theeseez'.

throughout -- thruhowt is unambiguous and preferable to the awkward triple vowel required in the too-specific enunciation 'throo/owt'. This is another instance of the saving grace of the principle of maximum elision.

trachea -- traekya but also pronounced by some as 'trekeea'. The plural 'tracheae' pronounced variously as '-ki/ee' or '-kee/ee' is pretentious and to be avoided in favor of 'traekyaz'.

trousseau -- truhsoe. Again a too hard enunciation leads to the unfavored 'troo-' not present in the original French.

unchangeable -- uncaenjabl, where all difficulties of the original – do we drop the silent 'e' in '-eable'? is it '-able' or '-

ible'? – are resolved unambiguously. The fully elided form 'uncaenjbl' will probably eventually replace the above, and does the job perfectly well. We have retained the 'a' in '-abl' out of timidity and for the sake of a unique prescription here.

unintelligible -- unintelajabl.

unsophisticated -- unsofistakaetd. The only question is '-tak-' or the more precise '-tik-'. The choice depends upon the speakers usage. When spelling -- remember that so are All Little Children.

usual -- uezhwul or uezhuel but not uezuel or
uezueel or uezhuewel all of which are too prissy.

vernacular -- virnakyalr although '-lir' is possible.

vulgarity -- vulgeritee.

weird -- weerd.

willful -- wilfuhl replaces this willfully difficult spelling.

wretched -- wrecid in my old dictionary, but we wouldn't quarrel with 'wrecad' or 'wrecud' or 'wrecuhd'. These conundrums are usually best resolved by the Ocam's razor of the principle of maximum elision, here giving 'wrecd'. 'Wreced' however seems stilted.

xenophobia -- zenafoebya.

Yom Kippur -- Yom Kipir or Yom Kipr.

zephyr -- zefr. Lets hear it for the Gipper!

Sec VII.3: Conclusions.

As we anticipated, Modular English makes spelling much easier but still not trivial. It also makes spelling and writing subservient to the spoken language. For that reason the spelling of a given word is not always definable in absolute terms as precisely correct or irrefutably incorrect. Spelling becomes a matter of accent, emphasis, pronunciation, and the writer's intent. Evaluating the spelling is ultimately a judgement of whether or not the writer has succeeded in the attempted communication. A critical part of this judgement must be based upon the amount of avoidable difficulty to which the reader has been subjected.

Two guiding principles have been valuable in rendering words into Modular English.

The first is the constant reminder of our fundamental purpose: Make the language easy for All Little Children. This is done by the 'modular' or building-block structure into which the language is recast. The building-blocks are chosen from among elementary monosyllabic words to define the fundamental task or tasks of each letter.

The second guiding principle has proven invaluable in eliminating ambiguities, complicated structures and ugliness: The principle of maximum elision. This principle has the result of 'softening' the language and of eliminating precise (prissy?) enunciation in favor of the way real people really speak. In this sense, Modular English abandons the former role of language policeman trying to enforce some standard of speech, an effort that was doomed anyway with the dominance of radio, TV and movies. That role is now in the hands -- or rather in the voices -- of people. The written word is just a symbol – hopefully easily recognizable -- of the spoken word. The elisions in writing, in the above example 'zefr', still allow the written word to be a perfectly effective reminder of the spoken word. Why should we ask for more?

CHAPTER EIGHT:
MODULAR ENGLISH: EBONICS? GULLAH?

Sec VIII.1: Why the Fear and Loathing?

Proposals for language reform invariably generate an incommensurate knee-jerk reaction in most people. Why this emotional response? We have tried long and hard in earlier chapters to show that reform has old and very respectable origins. These include leading contributions from Shakespeare, Samuel Johnson, Benjamin Franklin and Noah Webster, as perhaps the most revered.

Notice that the names stop about 200 years ago. Certainly new words are coined at a mind boggling pace -- whether from slang or science or other languages -- so there is no lack of change in the English language. The language almost hungrily assimilates new words from every source without fear or jealousy. But this is change only in the sense of growth; not change in the sense of reform. Pro-active changes to correct irrationalities, absurdities, obscurities, ambiguities and all the gratuitous difficulties that plague the language *are not made*. If they occur at all, it is only by the process of slow attrition in which words gradually fall from use.

When any such pro-active changes threaten to be effected they are met with a firestorm of protest, and protest of interesting origins.

Why this emotional response? What is the source of these hostile outbursts? Our suggestion is that it is a fear-rage syndrome emanating from heresyphobia, a morbid and near insane fear of radical challenges to official doctrine. Like Caesar with ancient Gaul, we analyze opponents of language reform into three groups, each with its own reaction:

(1) A class of people -- perhaps one third of the population -- completely secure in their favored socio-economic position and in their abilities to cope and even prosper in any situation. This group has great power and strong

voice and the resources, abilities and confidence to weather any storm. Their response -- if any -- to language reform will be calculated and from the pocket but not from the heart. There is no emotional outburst here, whatever the appearances.

(2) Another class of people -- a middle third -- whose only slightly favored socioeconomic situation depends on their arduously acquired credentials and their rather muddled educational skills. These were the proverbial C-students before grade inflation. A typical example would be an English teacher or a librarian -- the Bob Cratchits of this world. They have a very real reason to dread language reform because their knowledge-advantage is based on rote-learning of trivial conventions which *will change*. They *are indeed* threatened by a change in the rules which would completely shake if not shatter the foundations of their social, professional and economic lives. This group has loud voice -- including teachers' unions –- and will be vociferous and hostile to any language reform which *is a very real threat* to them. The threat arises not only from the change itself in the language, but also from the diminished status of professions based on a language expertise which will now be easier to acquire.

(3) Still another class of people -- another third -- would at first sight seem to be purely beneficiaries of language reform, and they might have been expected to be supporters of such proposals. These are people who have never mastered written language skills. This is not to say that they are illiterate, some in fact are avid and able readers. But as a class they have difficulty in writing and spelling which preclude vast areas of upper-level employment. This group has never had any benefit from the existing written language, in fact quite the contrary. They are the victims of it, although many do not admit this fact or even perhaps realize it. By a

120

process of rationalization that has been the dominant part of their psychology since grade school they have succeeded in excluding from their conscious minds the whole traumatic experience of the frustration and failure of their long and painful struggle to master spelling and writing. By a further process of avoidance, they are careful never to revisit such negative experiences. This group also includes many working-class minorities who have historically been ill-educated, and also many under-educated immigrants who use English as a second language rarely if ever spoken or read in the home.

However, to the very considerable extent to which they do have voice, *this third group too will be opposed to reform* even more violently than the second group. What they fear is a very real possibility. What they fear is a two-tier sociological-cum-educational *experiment* in which their children alone will be fobbed off with an ersatz version of the language which will *label* them and *handicap* them for the rest of their life *after the experiment is inevitably abandoned as a failure.*

This threat is very real and their fears are perfectly well founded. Any *failed* reform is going to leave All Little Children as victims in its wake.

The most important facet of Modular English now makes its appearance. It goes beyond the tactical details of any changes in spelling. The most important feature of language reform must be the strategic design of a fail-safe implementation program. We will propose just such an implementation strategy in a following chapter. But first we continue our discussion and resolution of controversies surrounding language reform.

Sec VIII.2: A Brief History of Ebonics.

A few years ago when the Oakland, California, School Board sprang a language reform proposal on an unprepared world, all hell broke loose in a spate of racist recrimination. The only surviving evidence of the event visible from this distance is the racist term Ebonics which is a derogation meaning Black phonics. Whatever actual plans the school board had to improve the educational performance of their students – who are predominantly Black, urban and poor -- were lost in the scuffle. What remains is the totally false impression summarized in 'Ebonics' as a disparagement of any and all language reform.

The motivation for the assault -- from *all* sides -- on the Oakland School Board' proposal was based on a series of spurious assumptions. These included:

(1) The pedagogically false notion that failure breeds success. If the children -- for whatever reasons, but my assumptions would be multiple including: poverty, cultural deprivation, lack of motivation, lack of successful role models, negative peer pressure, second rate schools, lack of pre-school and kindergarten preparation, lack of parental involvement, disrupted home life, TV, video games, basketball mania, insufficient use of rytalin ...... -- if the children can't do the work, make them! If they can't decipher 'thoroughly' and spell 'linguistically', make them practise or is it practice?...I don't know. Hit spell-check. Look it up. It's both or either or it depends on the time of day. What difference does it make? And who cares?....make them practice the assignments with the vocabulary that is used by all the Berkeley-bound rest of us. And also,

(2) The false notion that by reducing the complexity of the assignments and at least *starting* with something familiar to the students, the students would never advance beyond some street argot of 'Yo, bro' and 'aks'. Success breeds success. Start where they are and go from there. In any case the argot is a put-on designed to annoy adults, particularly up-tight white adults, and most specifically school teachers.

(3) In present day culture (or lack thereof) All Little Children get there vocabulary primarily from TV and

movies. Their verbal skills drive their writing and reading skills (again, or lack thereof) rather than *vice versa*. There is no hope of success for any dual agenda of teaching writing and reading skills to generate vocabulary. Vocabulary is obtained elsewhere. If there is a sensible dual agenda it must be to make the students as literate as they are verbal; and to get the students to read and write well enough to enjoy it as an alternative. The chance of winning many students back to the written word from all the hypnotic glitz of the electronic media is slim to none. We know exactly who to hold responsible for any vocabulary defects or shortcomings. It's the entertainment media greedily 'sloppin' the hogs' for the billions and trillions of profits, and no more concerned about the effect than is your friendly neighborhood drug pusher.

(4) The false notion that the reduced goal of learning to read and write the day-to-day vocabulary of the children, is going to degrade the language or the language skills of the students is to greatly overestimate the involvement of the less able students in the academic process. By the time children become behavior problems, usually around the 5th or 6th grade after failing to keep pace in the critically important introduction to the written language, they already feel rejected by the education system and have disconnected anyway.

The conclusion is that the written language is losing children in droves and cannot continue to be such a forbiddingly hostile experience. This hostile experience has completed its destructive work on the psychology of the less able students already by the 4th grade. It is imperative that we make the written language at the entry level and beyond much easier. Unless we do, an ever increasing gulf is going to open between the curriculum requirements and this sizable minority of less able, less prepared, less motivated, less supported, more distracted elementary school students. Once lost they are *not* gone forever. Many will reappear over and over again during the next 50 to 60 years of their lives as social, economic and at worst even moral and criminal burdens on society. Whatever investment we make to help them succeed as elementary school students will be repaid many times over when they then become productive and even prosperous full participants in the society. There is no more important change we could make to ensure elementary school success than to adopt Modular English.

But the real conclusion we wish to reemphasize here is this: the specter created by the Ebonics uproar that spelling reform contributes in any way to the degradation of the language is arrant nonsense. As we have demonstrated repeatedly in many examples from a wide spectrum of human endeavor, Modular English with its rationalized spelling is more than adequate to express any and every idea that can be spoken in English.

Sec VIII.3: Gullah -- A Valid Dialect?

Closely related to Ebonics by their racist overtones is the concept of Gullah, a degraded localized form of the language. In isolated English villages they were called regional dialects and were (and some still are) as different from the English that we know as Dutch or Swedish is from German, or Cajun or even French-Canadian French from the French of L'Academie Francaise. Gullah refers specifically to the dialect of former slaves isolated on the islands off South Carolina and Georgia, but also generically to that of former slaves as far afield as Guyana.

Here again, the accusation leveled against Modular English is that it will open the floodgates of degradation of the language to some inferior universal common denominator resembling Gullah dialects. These are portrayed (parodied?) in *Uncle Remus* stories as:

> One day atter Brer Rabbit fool 'im wid dat calamus root, Brer Fox went ter wuk en got 'im some tar, en mix it wid some turpentine, en fix up a contrapshun what he call a Tar-Baby, en tuck dish yer Tar-Baby en he sot'er in de big road,

en den he lay off in de bushes fer ter see wat de news wuz gwinter be.

This is surely a parody, however well intentioned. 'Turpentine' and 'contrapshun' are perfectly pronounced and out of place. What about the rest of it? First of all, there is no objection to writing this way if it is the way you speak and unselfconscious. It's perfectly easy to understand and unambiguous. Secondly, the author's intent to portray Gullah is easily translated into Modular English -- in fact with quite a few changes: 'Wun', 'sum', 'wot', '-baebee', 'tirpntien', 'kontrapshn', 'hee', 'roed', 'lae', 'nues' and 'bee'; some more complex and some less. But third, Gullah is not in any way a result of Modular English, even with the principle of maximum elision. Compare:

Wun dae aftir Bruthr Rabit foold him with that calamis root, Bruthr Fox went tuh wirk and got him sum tar, and mixd it with sum tirpntien, and fixd up a kontrapshn wic hee kold a Tar-Baebee, and took this heer Tar-Baebee and set hir in thuh big roed, and then hee lae of in thuh buhshiz tuh see wot thuh nuez wuz goeing tuh bee.

The appearance is not so different from Gullah, simply because Modular English is still new and strange. But in fact -- even with maximal elision -- Modular English gives the reader very specific marching orders. The 'th-'s in 'the', 'that' and 'this' are explicit; even elided to 'bruthr' the pronunciation is completely specified and traditional. 'To' is softened to 'tuh' but if the author wished a stronger enunciation it could be specified by 'too'. A problem crops up in 'bushes' – traditional in the original -- but 'buh/sh/z' in the completely elided Modular English form, which is awkward in appearance and could be the easier 'buhshiz'. It came as a surprise to render 'off' as 'of' (now consistent with 'if'), and 'of' of course becoming 'uv' in Modular English.

In any case, we have made our point. Modular English is at the command of the writer. If a Gullah dialect is wanted, a

Gullah dialect can be communicated to the reader. If traditional pronunciation with casual or vernacular enunciation is wanted, that can be indicated. If traditional pronunciation with strict or formal enunciation is wanted, that too is readily available. But Modular English *per se* cannot be blamed for any deterioration of the language. As we have demonstrated repeatedly and at length, Modular English has every bit as much capacity for every task as does traditional English.

Except one. If it is your intent to make life miserable for All Little Children, for all time; to deter them from reading and writing; to delay or even preclude their access to conceptual learning of subjects with *idea*-content; to relegate them to a lifetime of quasi-literacy and limited employment opportunities; to fill the streets and the slums and the welfare offices and the jails and the prisons with generation after generation of the debris of anti-socialized failures; if this is your intention, then traditional written English is your instrument of choice.

Sec VIII.4: Language -- Where From? Where To?

When a child begins to read at age 3 or 4 the active vocabulary is less than 100 words, most of them trivial monosyllables of the 'cat in the hat' variety. It is important to build slowly and securely on this base with an absolute sense of security for the child that the printed symbols *always* have the same meaning. But if the

> cat in the hat baked a
> cake and then sat down to eat it
> and found it to be too hot and had to
> wait two hours

then all hell breaks loose. What is this 'back-uhd'? Or the 'cack-uh'. OK so 'down' is something new and it rhymes with 'ow' but then why do we need 'found' instead of 'fownd'? Now 'cat' and 'hot' are OK and sometimes 'o' is like in 'toe', but where and what and why are 'to', 'too' and 'two'? So if we learn from 'toe' and 'cat' how to pronounce 'bake' and hence 'cake', then explain 'eat' and 'wait'. And on and on. There is a special rationalization -- no, that's an irrational use of the word rationalization -- there is a separate and distinct *new excuse* for almost every word. Count the exceptional cases in this childish phrase: I find at least 10!

Now obviously many children are able to take this in stride and retain all this at first glance and they -- perhaps a third -- never look back, never forget or need to be reminded of a special case once they've seen it, and race on to full literacy. For this elevated fraction, the world of reading, writing, and education of all kinds is a piece of cake. They are guaranteed to be the future mandarins of our society.

What about the rest? We don't need to analyze them for faults to find plenty of reasons for perfectly normal children to react with instinctive revulsion to such a Rube Goldberg construction as even this most elementary application of traditional English. In fact, the opposite question would seem to be more reasonable. We credit the group able to master and retain this proliferation of arbitrary rules as possessing a most valued and envied attribute -- high intelligence. And in many obvious ways this judgement appears to be correct: this is the way it is; the rewards are great; don't balk, don't argue, just go along to get along. If you can do it, it certainly is the sensible thing to do. The social pressures on All Little Children to succeed are so great that no one of them would dream of criticizing the subject matter they are being required to choke down.

No. They criticize themselves as being in various ways inadequate. And in the sense of being unable to conform to the demands put upon them they obviously are inadequate. But in another very real sense, blaming the difficulty of the work on the subject matter and not on the shortcomings of the student is the more intelligent thing to do. In the first place, it is an obviously true conclusion. There is neither logic nor consistency in the written language, nor any defensible reason or purpose for their absence. Furthermore, change is the creative and imaginative approach demanded by every ongoing problem. Little Children can't change their innate aptitudes. Rather than abuse All Little

127

Children of all successive generations by flogging them into submission -- or rather into repeated failure -- over this chaotic language, why don't we simply fix it.

We're like a person who persists in driving on a flat tire. It's true that you can do it – not very fast and not very far, but certainly without ever stopping – and you can even make continuous but arduous progress. But we all know better. Just pull over to the side of the road as soon as you can and fix it. The time and effort spent fixing a flat tire are repaid immediately by fast and easy progress for the rest of the journey. And there is an even more important reason for fixing it. Gimping along on a flat tire can destroy the wheel and do serious damage to the car resulting in major expenses.

This whole metaphor is played out with *every* child, including those who ostensibly succeed. Success may appear easy for some and be hard or even impossible for others, but it requires an inordinate amount of effort from everyone. If we would just stop for a moment and repair the flat tire of our written language, *everyone* could resume their journey without the restraint of having to learn a jillion picky rules about spelling and pronunciation. And we would minimize the irreparable damage done to the children -- All the Little Children!

The ones for whom traditional English would be easy will now find Modular English much easier. They can spend the time saved studying literature, history, psychology, mathematics, art, music, all subjects rich in ideas, culture and intellectual challenge and all more interesting than spelling and practice reading.

Those for whom traditional English would have been their *bete noire* are also free to go on to idea-rich subjects with their self-esteem undamaged by the gratuitous struggle and failure to navigate its treacherous waters. With their enthusiasm and optimism unspent, it is not at all obvious how this cadre of students will cope with such idea oriented subjects. Keep in mind -- *this experiment has never been carried out before.* In the past, each one of these students has carried the burden of failure since the earliest grades when they fell victim to the traditional written English language. They have been thoroughly brain-washed into the belief that they are intellectually damaged goods. No one has any expectations of them, least of all themselves.

It's like trying to make a tennis player out of a kid who has been cut from his little league baseball team. What you get is an apathetic 10 year old who is convinced that he is not an athlete and so why bother? In his mind the result is inevitably just another failure so to save himself any risk to his ego he refuses to make an effort. The truth is that *anyone* who plays tennis from age 10 is going to be a *very* good player. Maybe not for a profession but for a lifetime of fun and exercise. Age 10 is just too soon to judge people and certainly too soon to discard them.

And why judge? Why discard? We are so wealthy that we can afford any expense, however seemingly extravagant, to ensure a happy and productive life for any child. The price of a year in prison is vastly greater than that of a year of *any* education; the cost of an execution far exceeds the *total* cost of any education. Before we give up on any child we must remember these costs.

I am reminded of the notorious 11+ exams in the old British school system which selected boys for college track at age 11. We know better than that now, and try to keep all students' options open as long as possible and even have multi-tracks to higher education for late bloomers. But what real good can this effort do if we still figuratively beat the intellectual spirit, the very educatable life out of the very cadre which would have failed the 11+ exams. And we do that from the second grade through the sixth with the demand that they master the incomprehensible! Traditional written English. And now to make matters even worse we subject them to innumerable achievement exams presumably to flog them into greater effort. Is this not a *de facto* 11+ exam? To have such pressures on All Little Children in the unbelievably prosperous USA of year 2000 is just as cruel and counter-productive as were the tests which separated the educatable class from the laboring class in poverty-wracked Britain prior to 1950?

Many pedants will object that learning trivial and picky rules is essential practice for learning nontrivial rules which have real intellectual content. It teaches discipline, virtue, merit, hard work, and on and on. Hello! This is your friendly puritan speaking. I say baloney. The way to get engaged in the business of learning is to be interested. The way to get interested depends ultimately on a resonance in the mind, not on any servile practiced and acquired ability to conform to the demands of arbitrary authority. Little boys who can't read 'cat in the hat' can motor at full speed through dinosaurs and Pokemon wars. The difference is that they're interested.

Why should we place an artificial language barrier between All Little Children and meaningful subject matter? Humanists -- at least those who are innumerate to an extent that scientists are never illiterate -- object with some justification that analogous mindless barriers obstruct the road to numeracy. They cite long division, compound interest, logarithms, etc. as essentially boring and irrelevant impediments to the bigger picture of numeracy. I won't argue except to say that at least the rules of these boring exercises are consistent. For example, 5 times pi=15.707963... *every* time it appears, without exceptions. Should education in the sciences be more qualitative and 'broad-brush' for non-specialists? Without doubt. And even for specialists, we should eliminate petty detail. But science -- even with its many flaws and irrationalities -- offers *no* excuses for persisting in the use of the chaotic traditional English written language.

Going back to the childish example above with the 10 exceptional situations in traditional English, we find *NONE* in the Modular English translation where each resolution is underlined:

> kat in thuh hat baekt a
> kaek and then sat down tuh eet it
> and fownd it tuh bee too hot and had tuh
> waet 2 owrz.

There certainly are a number of rules applied but they are without exceptions. Once learned, always applicable. No exceptions? Not exactly. Not perfect but certainly orders of magnitude better than what we face with traditional English. You really have to *look* for problems of Modular English in places which All Little Children can reasonably avoid while they gain expertise, confidence and -- most important of all -- a love for reading.

Sec VIII.5: Concluding Remarks.

The first reaction to Modular English reform comes from people who have survived the ordeal of traditional English with some success. A standard response from these comfortably ensconced on the far shore is: 'I did it, so they can too.' In this world where nothing is simple or really as it might appear, even this trivial response requires closer examination. Lets grant that our respondent did indeed survive and even with flying colors. The first question that occurs is: 'What about those who didn't?'

My fading recollection of public school brings to mind old friends and acquaintances of lower to middle class small town America. There were few minorities and everyone spoke English as their native and only language. Even then the class of 100 students was divided into three parts: one third tough and unruly boys mainly from the lowest economic level who were regarded as uneducable; one third uneducable girls who were taught typing and home economics; and a third who were deemed worth preparing for university. The ones who came back to the 35th reunion were those who had something to brag about, and they had done very well: business or professional affluence, two houses, three cars, three kids, three grandchildren, winter and summer vacations, early retirement coming soon. The good life. The returnees were about one quarter of the class and -- with the exception of a few athletes -- were all from the university track. They all had positive recollections of their educational experience and had led exemplary but usually rather undistinguished lives. Surely these are the ones who 'did it'.

What about the rest? What about the ones sidetracked by the difficulties of the education process into less rewarded walks of life? Who speaks for them? Who analyzes the reason for the recalcitrance among the boys, or the apathy among the girls who were among the two thirds rejected by the education system before the eighth grade as being incapable of higher intellectual aspirations?

The partitioning of students in small town Canada of 1950 is remarkably similar in many ways to that of big city America of 2000. A recent graduating class of an outstandingly successful inner-city high school (Lamar of Houston) had about 1800 students again equally split into three groups: an academic elite who got all the recognition of honors, awards and scholarships to top-rank universities as well as the obvious adoration of the teachers; the analog of our old typing class now empowered with front-line skills in business applications of computers and headed -- with their families immense gratitude and relief -- for immediate employment; and the seemingly inevitable unruly boys headed for what? The divisions seem still to be made along socioeconomic lines but these also coincide closely with racial divisions. There are remarkable exceptions in both directions. Gifted white athletes who couldn't get into junior college, gifted black students who had to decide between scholarships to Harvard and Stanford.

All of this is sociologically very interesting. To reemphasize our primary point: two thirds of the students leave this elite high school in big city America in the year 2000 judged at some level as academic rejects and having consequent severe limitations on their career expectations. From my own personal acquaintance, I can state anecdotal evidence that some of these judgements were made not at Grade 11 or 12 but long before, and have been etched in stone since at least the sixth grade. The Harvard-Stanford bound had their literacy skills in place and continued to lead an academic life of uninterrupted positive reinforcement; the junior college rejects had already developed a negative attitude which will obstruct their progress all their adult lives. This negative attitude surely has many conceivable causes. Our point is unarguable: it coincides completely in occurrence and time of onset with written language difficulties directly attributable to the intractable chaos of the written English language.

The problem impacts across all socioeconomic, racial and ethnic boundaries. Can Modular English eliminate it? No, not 100%. I am not disputing the existence of a spectrum of learning abilities summarized in the notorious Bell Curve. There inevitably are going to be people who cannot be reached, people who *define* the left-hand tail of the curve.

But the evidence is that we are not talking about the left-hand tail. We are talking about something like one-half the students who are *damaged* permanently by the struggle with gratuitous and curable difficulties in our most elementary and fundamental means of communication. Essentially everyone has to struggle. Those who succeed are temporarily impeded, but having burst through the barrier are thereafter made the darlings of the education system. Those who struggle more, and begin to falter and fail, and whose abilities are brought into question and -- worst of all -- who begin to lose faith in their own abilities -- become the casualties and victims of the system. They never again can participate fully in the education process. They don't drop out physically but they do withdraw emotionally. All interests, ambitions and enthusiasms are curtailed by the fear of failure and further rejection. The evidence is that the negative impact of written language difficulties permanently damages the learning abilities of over half of all students.

Is it possible that they're just stupid? The answer does not depend on what the meaning of 'stupid' is, but rather on what fraction of the population we choose to discard. Because by labeling them 'stupid', even implicitly, the damage done is essentially that. We forever preclude them from whole-hearted participation in their own education. Full participation requires interest, enthusiasm and optimism; none of which are possible with the specter of this damning failure constantly lurking in the student's psyche.

CHAPTER NINE: EDUCATION FOR A CHANGING WORLD.

Sec IX.1: The New Millennium,
The Future of Mankind, and the Importance of the USA.

The speed of world change -- already at a breakneck pace -- seems to be ever accelerating. In order to maintain the economically favored position traditionally viewed as our birthright we must educate an ever increasing fraction of our ever growing population to an ever higher level in an ever larger array of ever more complex subjects. It is an awesome task. How can we possibly aspire to so much, let alone succeed.

It may seem that this is an irrational and even an impossible assignment to undertake; and that the reasonable view and really only fair goal for our society to adopt is to aspire to a comfortable equity with our world neighbors. After all, with the exhaustion of our natural mineral and energy resources we might succumb to a national funk of despondency and conclude that the golden age of American predominance has come and gone; we might be tempted to relax and enjoy a reduced position of world leadership, an adequate prosperity and a comfortable old-age for an aged society.

Such a state of nirvana can never be in equilibrium with the real world. It is clear that the future of humankind, however we might imagine it, will be disastrously *worse* if the US is not in an intellectual position to maintain its economic pre-eminence and thereby, ultimately, its power to enforce our ideals. This is not an attitude popular with our dependents world wide. Their anti-American attitudes are primarily based on the fact -- distasteful to ever admit even to themselves as individuals, let alone as separate nations -- that they are so dependent upon the US for a world order which respects the Rights of Man as set forth in the Bill of Rights and the American Constitution. These ideals are widely shared, but also widely violated. They are nowhere ultimately guaranteed except by the certainty of American power and will.

Worldwide resurgence of totalitarian states and a return to brutal and militaristic dictatorships of every magnitude is a constant threat. Without the power of the US to lead its weak, vacillating and pusillanimous allies to enforce a Pax Americana, this threat becomes a certainty. The danger posed by a weak America is quite literally a new Dark Ages, four hundred years of darkness and tyranny imposed on billions of people; in some areas by reactionary political or religious doctrines; in others by subsidence into deeper poverty exacerbated by disease, over-population and ignorance. We do not stand alone in protecting these ideals for mankind, but we do stand first and foremost, tallest and strongest. If we fall, all fall.

Sec IX.2: The Impact of the World's Poor; Free Trade and Open Competition.

The greatest inducement we have to *persuade* other countries to conform to our ideals of Human Rights is the promise to share our prosperity through free and open trade if they do, and the threat of economic sanctions if they don't. The resulting cheap foreign imports generate an economic boom for the upper socioeconomic classes, but -- at least directly -- economic redeployment of the undereducated working class. If we fail in that, the result will be unemployment and hardship which can erode the gains of the whole society.

Labor intensive industries go off-shore where labor costs are a small fraction of our own. The comparisons are dramatic: auto assembly line workers -- $30/hour in Detroit, $8/day in Mexico; garment workers -- $7/hour in South Carolina, $2/day in Thailand. The result is that whole industries disappear from the US -- steel and clothing are all imported -- and their home communities and work forces are devastated. Cars, electronics, shoes, truck farming all have been heavily impacted by free trade. To combat illegal immigration it is just a matter of time before labor -- as in the construction trades -- is defined as a commodity allowing even contract workers to enter under free trade agreements. All of these are inevitable by-products of free trade, and indeed of capitalism taken to its logical conclusion.

Not that capitalism is in any sense logical or consistent. We already solve shortages of computer programmers with immigration exceptions rather than salary increases, so it is inevitable that we do the same for all.

Even if one accepts -- as I do -- that free trade has a preponderance of beneficial results for all parties, there is one unarguable fact: the immediate direct effect of free trade is to put our least skilled and lowest paid workers in a direct and futile competition with their cheaper foreign counterparts. In fact -- from the above examples of auto assembly workers and steel workers, but also the example of electronics assembly workers and many more – this is also true of highly skilled, highly paid industrial workers; and is now also becoming a fact-of-life for intellectual workers in the new computer soft-ware industries.

Jobs -- bad jobs, good jobs, unskilled jobs, skilled jobs, manual jobs, intellectual jobs -- are being lost from the internal economy of the US. The argument is 'short term pain, long term gain', and eventually everyone gets a better job. What is presumed true is that the available jobs require higher skills and a better educated work force. What is probably true is that the pressures on people who are undereducated -- including those with too specialized skills as in the auto and steel industries -- are more onerous than ever before. What is unarguably true is that it is better to be a member of an educated elite which is insulated from the whole tough problem. We would wish for everyone -- our own loved ones most of all -- the very best education possible.

Is this beginning to sound familiar? We must not condemn a large fraction of our children to failure, alienation, under-education and a lifetime of paying for it. It is my contention that we do just that today to children age 4-10 when the alienation and/or apathy sets in following *de facto failure* to master elementary written language skills. The incidence of failure and the resulting destructive alienation can be greatly reduced by adopting our Modular English reforms to make rational and consistent the written English language.

Sec IX.3: Proliferating Demands.
The Curriculum Explosion.

Why is the present a time of crisis for the education process? Why can't today's kids do what we did? We mastered traditional English and prospered, why can't they? Are they stupid and lazy? Maybe it's the teachers. God knows with what we pay teachers and the way we abuse them, we don't deserve anything better. Certainly the written English language hasn't changed, so why is it that the students aren't learning ?

So many questions. We've discussed many and lets review the conclusions:

(1) Why now? As we have discussed, the fraction of children who swim, stay afloat or sink in the written language waters of elementary school have each always been roughly equal to one third. In the past it has been possible to ignore the importance of this evidence of difficulty. There was a much bigger range of opportunity for undereducated people in the closed economy of the past. Many job opportunities existed in areas where literacy of any extent was unnecessary: whole communities were founded on farming, logging, mining, fishing; large construction projects like highways, railroads, bridges, canals were much more labor intensive than now. Manufacturing was not automated so there were numerous literally manual jobs for men, women and children. The economy and peoples' expectations were so much reduced from today that relatively few women worked outside the home. Those who did were immensely curtailed in the limited number of jobs that were open to them: you could be a teacher, a nurse, a secretary, a clerk, a waitress, or a housewife. Teachers were required to have one year after high school, nurses three, the other jobs were open to everyone. Lack of education was so universal that it carried no stigma. Not that it was unimportant, it was. But there were so many extenuating circumstances that no one was judged solely on any educational limitations.

All of this started to change 55 years ago with the GI Bill to educate servicemen and women after World War II. The necessity for even greater emphasis on education came with the Cold War, and the arms race and space race with Russia beginning 40 years ago. After all these years of intense emphasis on the importance of education, the educated elite has become much larger, much more wealthy, and much more learned than ever before.

In all of these last 55 years the same fraction of elementary school children as today -- 1/3 to 1/2 – have struggled with spelling, writing and reading.

(2) But surely the standards have slipped. Why, I can remember ....in fact our memories are very selective. It *is* possible that some students aren't at the same level in some areas as in the past. But my recollection is of endless and mind-numbing repetition and -- most specifically -- of a very narrow curriculum. We never heard the words psychology, sociology, calculus, DNA, elementary particles, genetics, plate tectonics, politics, race, discrimination, evolution, drugs, addiction, STD's, Big Bang, criminology, computers, satellites, relativity, statistics, ... We never went to an art or a science museum, we never paid any attention to dinosaurs or to archeology. We did do a few things and do them well, but we arrived at university a very clean slate. So when we judge the level of accomplishment of today's schools, let's judge the whole package and not just their ability to do what we did. Because we did precious little. I didn't necessarily feel that way at the time, but looking back I am shocked to recall the low expectations. Is the present education better or worse? It is *different*, with not as much depth in the old fundamentals; but it is an immensely richer experience.

My conclusion is that the upper-schools could be an even richer experience except for the negative attitude of the alienated and marginalized students. If the childish enthusiasm with which All Little Children enter elementary school could survive the first six years, so that everyone entering middle and upper school could participate whole-heartedly in the process, then the whole education process could soar to immense new heights. But as things are now, with so many of the students rejecting the education process – as a result, in fact, of being rejected _by_ it -- we are destined to continue spending time, money and effort in a hopeless attempt to rehabilitate many students who 'cop-an-attitude' purely out of self defense and the conviction that has been impressed on them after five years of struggle with written English, that they are incapable of learning and face certain humiliation and failure if they try.

Sec IX.4: The Impact of Computers.

The initial impact of computers on the elementary education of little children is to add one more subject to the already crowded curriculum and one more distraction from reading to their lives outside the classroom.

Despite the undeniable long term gains realized through computers, the initial impact is to reduce the time and attention available for the classical study of reading and writing. Without continual reading at an ever increasing level, the child is dependent on the spoken word for vocabulary. There is soon a deep disconnect between the verbal vocabulary and the written vocabulary which can only be bridged by remedial reading. The result of reading at a level much lower than the speaking level is loss of interest in reading. This deep disconnect is naturally and easily bridged by Modular English, which is of course its fundamental purpose.

Childish play on a computer -- usually at the level of computer games -- gives a false sense of empowerment and is completely irrelevant to doing any actual useful _work_ on the computer. It is not even clear that such precocious computer exposure serves a real or a positive purpose. The presence of computers in the early grades is necessary to satisfy parents and politicians, but it is really too early to do anything substantial on the computer. What's the old saying? 'Familiarity breeds contempt.'

It is possible to use the computer as an online dictionary or encyclopedia, or as an atlas perhaps. All of these uses can just as well be done the old fashioned way, but in either case require a substantial ability to read the result, whether off the page or off the screen. More detailed information is available from a host of web-pages, which again require reading at a mature level. At this level of usage -- which is probably all an elementary school student could usefully do -- there is no qualitative advantage over looking things up in a book. Obviously it is at first a much more stimulating environment and an enriching and formative experience to use the computer. As for doing anything more sophisticated like arithmetic calculations or mathematical curve plotting, these can surely be dealt with no sooner than junior high school or even later.

Computers are surely in the elementary classrooms to stay. How useful that is remains a question. It is important to break down any emotional barriers and to give experience and access to children who might not get it otherwise. But what can they really be expected to do with it? It can be used as a library resource for looking up information, but is not essentially superior to books for this purpose; it can be used as a glorified typewriter and printer which is fine but not very instructive; it can be used to play games which is usually a mindless waste of time. To use the computer to actually *compute* -- as in arithmetic, as on a hand-held calculator -- is surely beyond the capacity of elementary school children.

Our tentative conclusions are these:

(1) Computers are in the elementary classroom to stay. The experience and resulting sense of empowerment are important.
(2) Computers require the same literacy as the traditional printed sources of information.
(3) Elementary or even middle school is too soon to use computers to actually compute.
(4) Computer games are a waste of time in the classroom or out.

Computers in the elementary classroom are a great novelty, stimulus and point of interest. Their *useful* use, however, requires the same literacy skills as mature books. The danger is that introducing computers too soon reduces them to a toy which distracts from focus on more fundamental matters. They are one more seductive competitor for classroom time which was traditionally spent mastering written English.

The world turns so rapidly! On re-reading these luddite reactionary remarks, I am amazed at myself. I now realize that my life as a physicist doing computer calculations for over 40 years has given me the much too restricted view of the computer as a tool for computation. Computers have no need for my defense and are obviously going to be an ever more dominating presence. This only makes the intellectual economy of Modular English an even more important necessity for modern education.

Having admitted all this, I _still_ maintain that the highest level of creative intelligence – which I would ascribe to some few poets, writers, philosophers, the deepest and most imaginatively creative scientists –- is not revealed on computers. What I would characterize as similar but more common forms of intelligence–- involved in qualitative judgements, moral values, human relations, effective decision making, leadership, communication, persuasion, debate, politics, economics, to say nothing of all art and music, ... –- all so integral to our humanity, but none exercised on computers.

Sec IX.5 The Media Blitz.

Perhaps the single biggest change in our lifetime has been the total dominance of TV and movies over our lives. The people of America are in total bondage to the entertainment industry. They dictate what we think about, how we talk and what we talk about, and how we spend our leisure time. Children under 18 in particular are totally enslaved by the sitcoms of TV which dictate -- but even worse, degrade -- how they speak, what they buy, what they want, how they dress, how they behave, and now even what crimes they commit.

It is useless to make excuses about extenuating circumstances: no one under the age of 50 watches the History Channel; children do not voluntarily watch Nova. So all right, some statistically insignificant fraction of all children under 18 might watch educational TV. The vast majority -- especially amongst the academic marginal performers -- do not derive anything educationally valuable from the entertainment industry.

The indisputable fact is that entertainment, most especially TV, has a gigantic negative impact on the amount of time children might spend reading -- it is hopeless to imagine them actually writing -- or studying. The vast majority of children spend their 'leisure' time in a passive spectator mode, not in an active and engaged performer mode. They *do not* read when they can idly watch TV. And they grow up to be adults who *do not* read. Ask the publisher of your local newspaper; ask the publishers of Life magazine, Saturday Evening Post, Colliers ..... Never heard of them? There's a reason. What is the average age of the readers of the surviving Time, Newsweek, New York Times, even Sports Illustrated and Playboy. Children do not read. If they are informed at all it is through sound-bites on TV news before they can switch channels to some idiot sitcom.

Whatever else the profiteers of TV and movies can claim for their media, they are well on their way to complete defeat of the print medium. The time spent reading by all children is constantly diminishing.

There are survivors. 1/4 to 1/3 of all children learn to read, write and spell without extensive practice. Some few more come from disciplined homes and ambitious parents where TV exposure is restricted and a regime of reading and homework is required.

The victims are the 1/3 to 1/2 for whom these skills are difficult and even somewhat unpleasant and painful to acquire. For this large number of children, TV and other entertainment -- for example music and sports as spectators not as participants -- are a path of least resistance, a pleasant diversion offering an uncritical and fail-safe activity. But what these non-activities accomplish is a permanent seduction of all these children away from reading and written language skills, which now have to be acquired solely in the classroom.

Is this really so different from times past? Perhaps not. Even then people for whom reading was a trial simply avoided reading which guaranteed that it remained as a permanent problem. They were then channeled into a low-performance education path with all the inevitable results. Two things have changed:

(1) We cannot afford to have almost half our children enter the modern economy without modern skills; and

(2) We cannot constantly increase the academic demands on children because the time available remains essentially just the classroom time. Thanks to the media monopolization and distraction, we can't count on children reading and studying outside the classroom. In fact this was always probably the case for most marginal performers anyway, so to do so is a *new experiment*. Our point is that these are *not* empty hours. They are filled with the freely available and all pervasive seductive and entertaining din of TV, targeted -- to make matters even worse -- at just this most susceptible population of those with learning difficulties.

Modular English with its easier accessibility to written language skills is the *only* way to reduce the demands of the classical curriculum without reducing the expectations; and thereby make room in the classroom schedule of elementary school children for subjects new and old with actual *idea* content.

Sec IX.6: Sociopolitical Importance of Modular English.

The only conceivable long-term cloud in the sky of US internal stability might be our inability to absorb large numbers of immigrants from Latin America and particularly from Mexico. The aim with any immigrant group is to switch their identification and allegiance quickly and completely by the second generation from their land of origin to the US.

The case of Mexico is unique for a number of reasons. The common border means that there can be a lot of visiting back and forth renewing family ties of the immigrant population. It is also financially advantageous for the elderly first-generation immigrants to retire back in Mexico, again renewing old allegiances. There is a third potential source of disruption in Mexico's historical land claims to much of the Southwest which could grow into a rallying point for separation. But the single most divisive influence which might divert the total allegiance of second- and later-generation Mexican Americans is their retention of Spanish as a first language. The resulting social, economic, cultural and educational gulf between Mexican Americans and the English speaking majority slows their full assimilation.

The move of Mexican-Americans to full English literacy will remove all such divisive distinctions. Modular English will smooth this transition by making elementary education much more accessible to Spanish speaking children. It will also defuse pressure toward bilingual education and an eventual bilingual division in the nation. In this respect, the Spanish language is very tough competition for English. It is much more phonic and – so I'm told – has a much less redundant vocabulary.

The importance to the future unity of the nation and to the individual Mexican-Americans of full socioeconomic assimilation are obvious to all concerned. The 50-year projection of the Mexican-American population as more than one third of the total US population make this problem acute. The poverty, insularity, under-education, and under-employment of this huge population is a threat to the nation's future even more certain than any separatist movement or even bilingual movement. Modular English is a huge step toward a more inclusive language maximally accessible to all.

Sec IX.7: Concluding Remarks.

The easiest and most natural reaction -- of everyone watching from the sidelines -- to the faltering scores on academic achievement tests is to criticize the children, and then their teachers, and finally their parents. All non-participants -- from the governor through the school superintendent and down to all the sidewalk superintendents -- love to recount how different it all was in their heyday when *they* were so on top of all the demands made on *them* that external exams were never even considered.

If true, this is certainly hard to understand. In my own recollection there were no head-start programs; my parents certainly read avidly but they never read *to* us; we started reading when we got to school in the first grade, not before; and we never ever had homework before high school and not much then. There were never any external exams until the 12th grade and then only for people going to college.

What we did have was a very limited curriculum with plenty of time for repetitive learning. The repetition and drilling were endless and boring and a turn-off for everyone. The teachers were of all degrees of dedication and ability. The children were from a spectrum of lower to middle class families who were literate but didn't seem to be manifestly ambitious for their children. Certainly there was no particular involvement or any real interference by parents in school activities. The attitude was one of *laissez faire* on all sides. The parents didn't push, the teachers didn't drive and the children didn't care.

Could it really have been this serene? To skip forward 30+ years to my own children's experience, I really believe the schools of the 1980's were not so different from those of the 1940's. The whole gigantic anxiety attack seems to be a recent affliction. Could it be that we should all back off and calm down and let children be children with time to learn and understand in a less frenetic atmosphere? Is there perhaps a self-defeating element in running schools from K through 12 as a never ending sprint to some finish line, whose sole measure of success is to memorize the answers for all multiple choice questions ever to have occurred on an SAT exam? We are guilty of robbing our children of their childhood. And with it, the pleasure of learning, the very *possibility* of understanding, and the pride of achieving. Every step is monitored and tested and criticized. Our children can hope to find no independent thought, initiative, self realization, or even basic happiness in school. And God help anyone who falters. God help those -- and they are not few -- who are weighed in the balance and found wanting, and never given a moments peace or respite, or a chance to simply *enjoy*.

My advice to everyone would be to simply calm down. We are living through a new age for the very *first* time, and we are not doing a very good job of it. Surely there must be a relevant oriental philosopher out there somewhere who can tell us to relax and enjoy, that less is more, that a serenity of spirit and a quiet heart will make us strong. Could it possibly be that what really matters in our young children's education is not *how much* they learn, or even so much *what* they learn; but rather that they learn *how* to learn. And the number one requirement for learning is *interest*. And a pre-requisite to interest in any subject is a confidence that one's efforts will be rewarded with success. Success of genuine understanding cannot be achieved by any shortcuts. Such success really needs time to focus and digest, to savor a subject and discuss it and turn it over in one's mind.

But the cry goes up: No time! No time! We have to get on with it. We have too much to do. To do what? If the children don't understand it and don't enjoy it, that is if their studies are not successful, what has been accomplished? Certainly nothing positive long term. Maybe a certain amount of undigested material has been memorized to regurgitate on the next multiple choice exam, but it is worse than a house of cards. When a house of cards collapses at least it does no harm to the cards. But when a child's mind is roiled with random disconnected undigested factoids, and then they find some variation required on the next achievement test, they are helpless and doomed to fail. Not only does immediate failure result but also permanent harm has been done to morale, and a loss of faith in deeply ingrained study habits. The ability to learn diminishes with each failure. Short term goals generate faulty learning habits which preclude long term success.

Can we ever go back to a quieter and less demanding time? I think the answer has to be no. Children are assailed with all sorts of information from a multitude of very insistent, intrusive and seductive sources. They have to be in the real world, even in the classroom. The education process has to include at least some of the excitement of the new hyper-information age. How can the education process accommodate all these demands?

Some kind of compromise has to be reached between the classical in-depth study of a very restricted curriculum and the *irresistible* pressure to learn something about everything in the burgeoning new world. We cannot expect to just add and add and add new demands on children, without subtracting something. Nor can we postpone confronting the real world until elementary education is complete without losing the children's interest, respect and attention. It is a serious dilemma which demands serious change. One great need is for knowledgeable and talented people to involve themselves in elementary education, so that attractive and valid views of modern topics can usefully be presented even at elementary levels. All Little Children love the Big Bang.

Another great need is for teachers of classic subjects like language and mathematics to acknowledge that they can no longer monopolize the students' time and energy to the same great extent as in the past. They must be able to achieve acceptable goals in fundamental skills more efficiently. This means less time, less repetition and fewer failures. One way to do this is to reduce the level of the goals. A better way -- which is the aim of Modular English -- is to retain the same level of expectations but to make the path leading to them easier and more productive.

We must streamline, modernize and rationalize the elementary written language education requirements so that all students can master them with less time, effort and trauma. The ever increasing demands put on students by the mass of new ideas, new subjects and new skills essential in the modern world have crowded the curriculum to the point that the intricacies of the written English language can no longer be tolerated. We are wasting our resources of time and money, but most important of all we are wasting our most precious resource -- literally the hearts and minds of All Little Children -- by our stubborn insistence on teaching them a written English language that has been recognized since the time of Benjamin Franklin to be an obstruction to learning.

CHAPTER TEN: POST-TRAUMATIC STRESS DISORDER FROM SPELLING?

Sec X.1: Changing the World. Foes Become Friends.

The knee-jerk reaction to any suggestion of English language reform -- even from its advocates -- is that it's 'pie-in-the-sky', 'pipe-dreaming', 'you-can't-get-there-from-here' stuff. Of course this is over and above the *violent* reaction from its opponents. They become apoplectic at the mere thought of desecrating their God-given patrimony of traditional English. They blithely ignore the fact that even 'traditional' English has changed many times -- as written by Shakespeare, defined by Samuel Johnson and revised by Noah Webster and their successors. And it is changing today, but too stubbornly slowly to benefit whole new generations of its victims.

The attitude of language reform opponents is the same as that of reactionary people of every stripe -- they are, after all, the very same people -- just digging in their heels to instinctively oppose one more change for the better. Their hysterical response to change is universal and rooted in fear and paranoid delusion.

The fear is that they will lose the hard-won security and distinction which they regard as the right of their small elite group who are specially chosen to save the world. And save the world from what? from who? Why from the mass of common people -- i.e., the rest of us -- whose base instincts, whose gluttonous and perverted appetites and whose unprincipled and amoral predilections will lead direct to an instant replay of Sodom and Gomorrah. Their fear is of the future, and Sodom and Gomorrah is a very real possibility if we refuse to make the changes essential for progress. But not a seductive Sodom and Gomorrah of excess, luxury and pleasure; rather a degraded Sodom and Gomorrah of ignorance and poverty, overpopulation, disease and world-wide repression. The only salvation is in education and economic uplift for the whole world's population.

Their paranoid delusion is not that there is a small elite group; but that they -- the vast majority of reactionaries -- are part of it, or even on the fringe of it. They are in fact the lower-middle class who feel a threat to their marginal advantages over the poor, the under-educated, the under-employed, the servant-class of our modern society. It will be a strange alliance, with the National Rifle Association from the far-right sharing the barricades with the National Teachers Union from the far-left; and all those from the middle whose precarious pretensions are based on their facility with the arbitrary rules and the impenetrable maze which _is_ the traditional written English language.

The one tie that binds all those instinctively opposed to language reform, who are natural enemies to all reform, the tie that binds them to the cause of language reform _as advocates_ must be the admission in their hearts that either they or someone they love, or both, have been permanently scarred by the elementary school experience of trying to master the traditional written English language. Once we can get everyone to admit that they have been hurt by the suffering and alienation – theirs or a loved one's -- resulting from the irrational demands of reading, writing and spelling traditional English, then _everyone_ will support Modular English reform with heart and mind and action.

Sec X.2: The Magnitude of the Task.

So how _can_ we ever change the written language of all 1.5 billion English speaking people? It could well be the most daunting task ever confronted. To lead people to such a radical change of such an entrenched orthodoxy would surely take the vision of Martin Luther combined with the leadership of Martin Luther King. It really _is_ a reform resembling the Protestant Reformation: we accept the basic value of what is being taught and simply want to make it most easily accessible to all people. It is comparable to translating the Bible into English so it can be read by everyone and not just by a priesthood schooled in an arcane language -- Latin in the old Catholic church, vestiges of medieval English which still abound in traditional English in the present situation.

151

We don't have another Martin Luther or another Martin Luther King, so we must find a way to accomplish our own reformation without such charismatic and inspirational leaders. 'How to do this?' is the question. Accepting all the arguments that it should be done, how can we do it?

We have a number of comparably monumental problems. One which comes to mind unfortunately raises the specter of racism which is not in question in the need for Modular English reform. <u>Every</u> family has loved ones for whom reading, writing and spelling are easy; and right beside them siblings for whom it is not, and for whom the educational experience is a never ending struggle and frequently a tragic disaster. <u>Every</u> family is involved.

Now let me construct a metaphor for language reform which *does* (at least in my reading on the subject) appear to involve race. The metaphor is the decriminalization of marijuana possession for which a disproportionate number of young Black males serve prison time. Efforts to decriminalize this rather innocuous transgression have taken years and are still work in progress. In spite of nearly universal agreement that the punishment does more harm than the crime, nothing is done unless the jails are overflowing.

Consider next a transgression which is <u>*overwhelmingly*</u> more dangerous and leads to *incomparably* more fatalities: that is drunk driving. When was the last time a white teenager served two years for having an open beer can in his pick-up? When was the last time a city judge was jailed on the way back to court after a three martini lunch? When was the last time an alcoholic River Oaks socialite was jailed for slowly and carefully and drunkenly and for the third time gliding without pause through a stop sign? It never happens! Why not? Because everyone is involved, everyone has sympathy and by a general consensus these crimes are decriminalized. Punishment would impact the politically powerful not just the politically impotent, so the law is changed *de facto* if not *de jure*.

How does all this have anything to do with the inability to master the reading, writing and spelling of traditional English? Hang on, we're there at last.

Because the inability to read, write and spell is at worst a small crime, a minor transgression, a misdemeanor whose only victim is the transgressor himself; and yet we punish it with draconian ferocity. For six years and more the transgressor-victim is repeatedly forced into the situation of failure, frustration and humiliation. All of this is done -- of course -- with the best intentions in the world, with the victims *real* interests foremost in our hearts. If only they would try a little harder, focus a little better, remember a little more a little longer ..... then what?

And some do. For what purpose? The fortunate ones can find a comfortable safe place in their family business where the real work is schmoozing the clients on the golf course anyway; and there are people hired to run the spell-check on the computer. So it was all for naught in this lucky circumstance. For those not so fortunate? Well there are places for them too where personality, initiative and other worldly attributes can carry them. In fact, even without all the nagging and suffering, they would have landed on their feet in the self-same situations.

And many don't. With what consequence? We are a wealthy and generous society so there is a whole spectrum of opportunities. But without being an able and confident reader, writer and -- most important -- *test-taker* a person can give up all hope of many aspirations: college, professional school, politics, any executive-level civil service position, police academy, military officer or NCO; any future including supervisory responsibility. It certainly isn't the end of the world, but it is a much tougher world.

So, you might well ask, where is the draconian punishment? Nothing really happens except to 'separate-the-sheep-from-the-goats'. Surely people will find their appropriate levels in any case.

I'm prepared to admit all that. But then the question must be asked: Why did we force All Little Children through all this suffering in the first place? If it doesn't _really_ make much difference, then it _really_ doesn't matter. And if it really _doesn't_ matter, then let's not do it. Why not?

Sec X.3: An Impossible Exercise for _YOUR_ Imagination.

Because the price is high. And the highest price of all is the impact on elementary school children -- the immediate and progressive alienation at least 1/3 of the students, remember -- who can't cope with the work. The first reaction of the smallest children is bewilderment that their sweet efforts are rejected; followed by apathy, fear, hopelessness and despair. They are being required to play a game for which they have no talent, in which they never succeed let alone excel. A game whose rules are beyond their comprehension for the simple but unacknowledged reason that they _are_ beyond comprehension, that is to say, they _**really are**_ incomprehensible. In fact, they are not intended to be comprehended, or understood; they are intended to be memorized and obeyed as by slaves. Is it any wonder that many little children get no pleasure from this game, they see no purpose in it, and they see no future in it for themselves? And is this what we extol as education? Is this the learning facility that is the 'open sesame' to affluence and status in our society?

As these demands continue and even escalate, this cadre of students has no choice but to fight back, which they do: through disruptive behavior in the classroom, by belittling and rejecting the whole learning process, and eventually by a permanent psychological disconnect from any participation in their own attempted education. Their reading and writing skills lag farther and farther behind those required for higher learning; so finally they are permanently disqualified from traditional studies based on literacy. The symptoms of alienation are flaunted almost gang-style by children and teen-agers who have failed, been rejected and finally discarded, _**and they know it**_. They feel hopeless with no recourse but to 'shoot-the-finger' at society. And they are right, and who can blame them.

Imagine how we -- the comfortable, successful and secure who were in the welcomed half of all children, those with the aptitudes and skills (and encouragement, preparation and motivation) to make literacy easy — would feel. Imagine a topsy-turvy world where these all counted for nothing. Suppose that from the very start there was nothing we were required to do that we were any good at. Suppose that art, music, voice, dance, athletics, gymnastics, physical beauty -- pick any two, or like me all, in which you rank in the bottom third of all humanity -- were the criteria by which we are judged *and therefore judge ourselves*. Not now as adults secure in our niche which we have carefully chosen and closely circumscribed to conceal our shortcomings even from ourselves; but then, as little children of 4,5,6: fat, awkward, clumsy children would be required to pirouette en pointe all morning every morning for five years until eventually, although no one said very much, it was clear to everyone (including the child, remember) that the attempt was hopeless. And in the afternoon, every afternoon for five years, there would be voice lessons. And finally, that too for most would be recognized as hopeless and stop.

How would we feel after such a failure, after being cast aside in this way? Would we pick ourselves up -- relatively unscathed, secure in our own self-worth — and go on with a life so stupidly interrupted? It is impossible to imagine from our mature and secure vantage point of a lifetime spent in the educated elite. Even with our extremely modest or even limited professional and material accomplishments -- with all evidence to the contrary notwithstanding -- we all think we're pretty damned good, and very smart in our own very special way even if we don't choose to show it all the time. In fact we're almost impregnable, and can't imagine feeling any other way.

In a word, we **can not imagine** what goes on inside All Little Children who can't meet the demands of elementary English. Now we have to imagine that this all-encompassing hostile experience has by the age of 11 occupied half a lifetime with no end in sight. And there *is* no end. The shock, frustration, despair, apathy, fear, disaffection, alienation, hostility and in many cases even violence of the afflicted children become permanent personality traits.

Sec X.4: Post Traumatic Stress Disorder in Half the Children.

We characterize these permanent negative personality changes as a form of 'Post Traumatic Stress Disorder'. The psychology profession has a much more narrow definition limiting PTSD to the stress of isolated but extremely intense life-threatening events. Elian Gonzalez's initial experience -- watching his mother drown and spending two days alone in an inner-tube adrift in the Atlantic -- is a prototype of such an event. Another common example is physical child-abuse, particularly rape and incest. We expand the definition of causative stresses -- validly we are convinced -- to include not just intense physical stresses suffered in a catastrophic incident, but also primarily emotional stresses suffered repeatedly over a much greater time. The emotional stress of repeated incest distinguishes it from rape in this respect, because violence and a singlular catastrophic event of very real physical mortal threat are not usually an element of incest. Another extreme example included in our definition would be brainwashing -- a process of emotional abuse explicitly designed to break down and restructure the victim's whole personality.

A third example is the stress accompanying confinement. Studies of the psychological reaction of WWII prisoners of war show a threshold effect: confinement under even extreme conditions for less than two years seemed to do no permanent damage; for more than two years the incidence of personality change was widespread. Senator John McCain appears to be one who recovered marvelously from the effects of his confinement during the Vietnam War, but in his autobiography recalls '' I couldn't control my despair. All my pride was lost, and I doubted I would ever stand up to any man again. Nothing could save me.'' Nonetheless, his political opponents did question his emotional stability, aware of the risk he had suffered of lasting psychological damage. The predominant reaction to extended confinement has been a loss of optimism and a lapse into apathy, hopelessness and depression -- victims blaming themselves for their externally inflicted helplessness and degradation. Mature men at the peak of their physical and mental and psychological powers -- such as 25 year old airmen -- suffered permanent loss of hope after more than two years of powerlessness. For many, the basic act of survival permanently exhausted them and they could never again summon the energy for another great effort. Why the contrast with McCain? One can't generalize from an individual and clearly exceptional case, but it is possible that McCain benefited from the WWII and later experiences by getting appropriate therapy for a recognized trauma. Little children traumatized by their negative experiences in elementary school receive no such help.

Examples are all around us. A typical scenario is illustrated by the microcosm of child athletics; but is also familiar in music and mathematics where precocious *individual* performance skills also excite a lot of simplistic dreams of grandeur (not all of them in the performer). These dreams are almost always frustrated by adult reality, and what replaces them? Frequently nothing. The child-star-performer's whole self-worth has been predicated on a failed enterprise! These widely admired but almost always ill-advised, all-consuming and grandiose dreams are replaced by a 'been-there, done-that, never-again' resolve not to get burned again. What can a failed celebrity do for an encore? Each of us seems to have one heroic episode within us, and when it is spent we fall exhausted.

Claims of Post Traumatic Stress Disorder are always met with skepticism. Show us your scars! This lack of understanding can only be the result of assiduous denial by the skeptics. Who among us does *not* suffer from PTSD? To anyone who answers 'I don't', I have to suggest 'You probably should'. Whose life has been so uniformly on the ascendancy that they have never felt failure? Who has never over-reached in their aspirations -- whether intellectual, professional, romantic -- and been denied after total commitment to a huge effort? And had to set lower and more realistic goals; to tackle problems of a magnitude more suitable for our mediocre talents; to accept our limitations *only after* an immense struggle? In a word: Who has not been forced to rationalize his failures and inadequacies? And if the answer is still 'I haven't', then I have either to admit

'You're a better man than I am, Charlie Brown' or to repeat that you are probably in deep denial. Because there has to be *something* out there that you wanted but couldn't have, that you've given up dreaming of for the sake of peace and comfort and sanity; there has to be something that you've decided isn't worth the effort; in fact something that is beyond you regardless of your best effort. And choosing that path of less resistance, making that rationalization, accepting as inevitable *your* reality, avoiding a struggle finally acknowledged *by you* to be hopeless *for you* is a form of Post Traumatic Stress Disorder.

These judgements constantly jostle us back onto the narrow reality paths of our existence. We read a few pages of philosophy without comprehension. The reality is that we are not smart enough. The well practiced rationalization is to disdain it as vacuous babble by some arty intellectual who doesn't have our grasp of practicalities (which we can't articulate even to ourselves). We embark on a new field of study. Like an ant probing a new terrain, our feelers are constantly asking the question 'What's out there *for me*?'. If the implicit and instinctive decision is 'Nothing' we again find ways to disdain it. String theory? Decision: 'Complicated nonsense by a bunch of charlatans'. Reality I: 'I have no hope of mastering these abstract mathematical skills, and I will never be able to participate'. Fifteen year old Rationalization: 'If I had 5 years to invest, I could understand it'. Reality II: 'I am too old, too lazy, too stupid, too ignorant and too pessimistic'. These are the survival strategies of the educated elite meeting something beyond their abilities. What can we expect from 7 or 8 year old children, already 2 years into their trauma?

PTSD personality damage precludes *any* whole-hearted, open-minded, enthusiastic, **_optimistic_**, and therefore any **_successful_** participation in further academic education. Every such enterprise threatens the student with a repetition of earlier traumatic experiences of frustration and failure which they are resolved to ward off by striking first. Some form of disengagement and withdrawal is begun by every traumatized student who then looks for moral support in kindred spirits. One of the earliest manifestations is disruptive behavior of middle school classes.   Alienated pre-teenage boys become actively hostile with the first testosterone surge and have to be separated from educatable students, but not before a chaotic period in the 7,8,9th grades where it is probably illegal to isolate them.   By high school there are various ruses of honors classes -- just as there were 50-60 years ago -- to provide a quiet positive learning environment for the favored few.

Recently attempts have begun to rehabilitate traumatized upper-middle class progeny and make them academically (i.e., socially and economically) acceptable.   These ruses include academic distinction for extra-curricular activities like cheer-leading and athletics, under the rubric of 'leadership' and 'community service'.   It's a positive first step to decriminalize learning-limitations, and it's being taken because significant numbers of the victims of our education system are at last being recognized among the off-spring of the politically powerful.

Sec X.5: Teaching for Learning or for Testing?

So -- again -- what has been lost?   These children have repeatedly demonstrated low aptitude; that we've done the best we can for them is the usual assumption.   Put them in some non-academic trade school where they belong and everyone get on with life.

This might be so.   And any difficulty in written English might be just the first symptom of a general inability to learn. We might be blaming the messenger for the message.

If you choose to believe this then there is nothing to be done. We live in the best of all possible worlds for the simple reason that it is the *only* possible world.   We might as well get used to the 'facts-of-life' and accept the inevitable results.   One of which is the alienation of one third of the children who enter the education process ***BEFORE THE AGE OF 11!***

This is actually an interesting manifestation of Heisenberg's Uncertainty Principle in a social context: The very act of measurement affects the quantity we are trying to measure and therefore precludes an accurate measurement.   Here the quantity being measured is the ability to learn.   A positive result is greeted with positive reinforcement and encouragement, resulting in increased self-confidence in the child being measured. A negative result also tends to be a self-fulfilling prophecy.

One question to ask is whether -- as the child is convinced -- or not -- as I believe -- the test _really_ measures the intrinsic ability to learn. If not, then any spurious negative indication has done lasting harm. In either case, any subsequent measurement -- valid or not -- is going to be accompanied by an anxiety attack for those who started badly. It is clearly an unstable situation that could be fatal to the child's morale and ability to perform. This is a very familiar syndrome in athletics: children have to be shielded from confidence-damaging negative experiences until they have built up a strong reserve of self-esteem and commitment. Losing -- especially in humiliating circumstances such as to someone smaller and younger -- can kill a child's interest immediately. And once an athlete loses a positive attitude, winning is practically impossible without a lengthy rehabilitation. And the damage is like a knee injury, it's never the same again.

An even more relevant question to ask is: Just exactly what is it we're trying to do? How did a language lesson turn into an IQ test? Surely that was not the original intent. Surely the intention was to enable All Little Children to get on with their education. What happened?

I maintain that perfectly acceptable intelligences -- even admirable and enviable ones, and especially those which are deep and creative -- can *and do* rationally reject the arbitrariness and inconsistency of the written English language. Anyone with an independent, enquiring, critical and logical mind, in fact, could well decide that it's a fool's game with no rules, no sense and no intrinsic interest. This kind of intelligence -- highly valued, for example in the sciences, as a heuristic, discovery-oriented, broad-band, synthesizing and innovating mode of thinking -- is completely ignored and even squelched by the nit-picking memorization required to master spelling (or elementary arithmetic as far as that's concerned).

And don't think that facility in this more subtle mode of thought will be found by multiple-choice quick-answer computer-graded IQ tests or SAT exams or GRE's either. Two of the greatest creative intellects in the history of science were Einstein and Bohr. Their debates began the deepest understanding of quantum theory. But don't visualize their dialogs as *snap-crackle-pop*, thrust-parry-riposte. In fact they were as far from that as possible. They spoke painfully slowly, and sometimes wouldn't respond at all until thinking about something overnight. Where would these great minds have ended up in our current education system?

Sec X.6: Concluding Remarks.

The real purpose of teaching elementary reading, writing and spelling is to teach reading, writing and spelling. What transforms it into a barrier to learning are the gratuitous difficulties of incomprehensible spelling conventions. These contribute nothing to the thought content of any word. What they do is completely divert the learning process into a senseless exercise in rote-memorization; and degrade the learning process, which surely must be about ideas and not vacuous factoids like '-ible' versus '-able'.

But by far the most serious condemnation of written English as it is now required, is that it is so destructive to the ultimate learning ability of so many children. Not many of these children, admittedly, are incipient Einsteins or Bohrs. But they are being permanently discouraged from even trying to learn by the artificial barrier of the conventional language. Even if some were such potentially great thinkers, we would never know it and would alienate them too. There *is* this different *qualitative* form of intelligence that is completely ignored by the current system of detail-oriented, memorization-oriented, idea-empty form of learning necessitated by traditional written English.

In the name of mercy to All Little Children, let's change it; make it softer, more pliable and more permissive. Instead of correct and incorrect, we would be better served with a spelling that could run the gamut of excellent, good, acceptable and difficult. Spelling would become a creative act, an act of judgement. Spelling could be interesting, a subject of discussion and debate, a matter of opinion. But its absolute demands should be relaxed and reasonable results should be recognized as valuable. Not so different from making change: get the dollars right, and hopefully the quarters and dimes, but don't sweat the nickels and pennies.

It will not escape anyone's notice that teaching this kind of written language is much more difficult. Just grading spelling tests becomes an intimate task requiring thought and judgement not just right or wrong. Teaching reading however becomes a much more systematic task based on a finite number of phonetic sound modules. Every word will be phonetically decipherable, which they now are not, hence the widespread antipathy to phonetics. How can we, how *could* we, how -- for so long -- **_DID_** we tolerate a written language disconnected from the accompanying -- and surely the *primary* -- spoken language.

CHAPTER ELEVEN: IMPLEMENTATION OF MODULAR ENGLISH REFORM.

Sec XI.1: Implementation Strategy.

The essential ingredient for successful implementation of the Modular English reform is a lucid public debate. We need access to the media and a loud clear credible voice to speak out for the cause. Loud we got plenty of. Clear we can order up. Credible is not so easy.

My choice is Barbara Bush who already has an admirable record as a literacy advocate and is one of the most widely known and loved and respected public figures in America. But her fight for literacy -- although admirable in every traditional respect -- has been incremental and quantitative. We need her help to make a revolutionary *qualitative* advance, not to wage the war from foxhole to foxhole taking tremendous casualties all the while; but to change the whole paradigm of the struggle: literally to make literacy universally *possible* by making the language *rational*, *reasonable*, *accessible* and *fair to all who wish* to learn.

Why did I just add the gratuitous 'who wish to learn'? Old habits are hard to break. Judge people as 'good' or 'bad', 'sheep' and 'goats', 'you live' and 'you die'. Each of us -- or is it only me – has this tiny little incipient Nazi Gauleiter deep inside eager to spring to attention with a 'Sieg Heil'. ***EVERYONE*** wants to learn!

How 'fair'? If you can talk, learn the 25-letter alphabet, learn about the same number of defining little 'module' words, and remember two cardinal rules:

(1) an 'e' immediately following a vowel means the 'hard' vowel so 'ate' and 'eight' are spelled 'aet'; and
(2) spell as you speak but -- please -- don't speak in a prissy way.

How 'accessible'? There will no longer be any absolutes in writing English. Communication is the key. You either communicate well, or perhaps you could communicate better; but you do *not* do it *wrong*. If communication does not occur, the onus must be shared between the communicator (the little child trying to express his thoughts) and the communicatee (the adult monitoring and criticizing those thoughts). Everything must be a work in progress and a matter of judgement, discussion and debate.

It will be a new time, like the beginning of democracy in the world at the introduction of debate in the Athens assembly in the reforms of Solon, around 510BC. And just as the human spirit soared in ancient Greece, we can anticipate that All Little Children will find voice, form opinions and develop confidence in the value of their own thought-processes. This does not happen now for the majority of little children in the current dictatorial-perfectionist mode of learning. The results inhibit people all their lives -- not from thinking and forming opinions -- but from expressing those opinions and from having a full free confident voice. From engaging in debate and argument for the simple fun of it, but also for the sake of smoothing the rough edges off their ideas in the ball-mill of discussion. People do talk but in guarded and non-committal and hence trivial ways which protect their thought processes from 'teacher's' condemnation of it being 'wrong'.

How 'reasonable'? If you can say it, you can write it. Uniquely? Of course not. There are innumerable versions of spoken English: regional, ethnic, individual, and even occasional differences of enunciation, emphasis, elision, accent, vocabulary. Some of these differences are almost unrecognizable as English. Ironically, some of the most egregious of these are found in England itself, even in London. The written language *can* and *should* represent these differences.

How 'rational'? Modular English requires a universal agreement that we all use the same 'modules' -- a set of elementary words -- to define *uniquely* the role of each letter of the alphabet. Obviously, this requires some re-definitions and many changes from the present chaotic spelling conventions.

With these basic modules in hand, the spelling of more complex words becomes an 'assembly' process, rather than the traditional 'spelling' one letter at a time. Is the 'assembly' process unique? No. Is it easily analyzed by everybody? Yes.

Our first implementation strategy will not include any fall-back positions for unforeseen failures. We proceed on the assumption that Barbara Bush is in place as President of the American Literacy League; so she is the President of A.L.L. She will be the symbolic leader of all and leader in fact of a governing structure modeled after the U.S. presidency, with a cabinet to do her bidding, to advise her, and to manage task forces in various areas.

As possible cabinet posts and exemplary candidates for each, we list the following:

(1) Vice President and Secretary of Television and Media – Oprah Winfrey
(2) Secretary of Print Media -- Elizabeth Sulzberger Hollas.
(3) Secretary of Computer Media -- Bill Gates, Jr.
(4) Secretary of the Treasury -- Bill Gates, Sr.
(5) Secretary of Federal Government Liaison -- Secretary of Defense William Cohen.
(6) Secretary of State Government Liaison -- George Prescott Bush.
(7) Secretary of Local Government Liaison -- President William J. Clinton.
(8) Secretary of Corporate Liaison -- Michael Jordan.
(9) Secretary of Education Liaison -- Secretary of State Margaret Albright.
(10) Secretary for Campaign Coordination – Secretary of Energy Bill Richardson.

Sec XI.2: Why Bill Gates?

Why would we want Bill Gates, Jr.? Money of course, if he has any left by that time. Why would he want us? To be loved. We do have a very symbiotic situation here where everyone directly involved can benefit tremendously, not in a material way, but in the only way that matters -- spiritually -- by doing lasting good.

Bill Gates has already attained the stature of a Henry Ford, or an Andrew Carnegie, as an historic industrial giant who has literally created the modern economy and in many respects defined the modern world. What remains -- if he has the vision to do it -- is to transform and modernize the world's culture by transforming and modernizing our language, and actually *defining* the world's means of communication to become Modular English.

The very suggestion that the world should have one overall language for universal communication, raises wails of protest and screams of anguish from the reactionary traditionalists who fear the loss of thousands of ancient languages and all their accompanying cultural heritages.

It's too late to bemoan the loss of cultural diversity, because it has already happened with emigration from farm and forest hut to village to town to city; with the economic necessity to streamline children of diverse ethnicity into one dominant educational system. In one elementary school in Houston, Texas, over 23 different primary languages were identified amongst the students. Does anyone believe that their grandchildren will be fluent in anything but English? Spanish might survive because it's being constantly refreshed by Latin-American immigration; Chinese and Japanese families fight the good fight with special schooling but this becomes a thin veneer for most after a second or third generation; Jews have a special incentive because of the historic threats to their very existence, to hold especially tight to their religious and cultural identities, but many fear even for this under the pressure of intermarriage and secularization. These separate cultures will survive only in organizations analogous to the Goethe Institute, or in academic specialties, or -- in a state of slow but inevitable decline -- in various ethnic religions. Cultural diversity will go the way of the buffalo herds and the redwood forests.

So the question is not *if* we are going to have a universal language; nor *what* the universal language will be -- although some doubt still exists for the long term (circa 100 years) because of the prospect of a totalitarian regime in a fully modernized and industrialized but still regimented China. It already *is* English. The only *real* question that remains for the foreseeable future is whether English is going to be a help or a hindrance. In its present *written* form we hope to have convinced you that it is a hindrance. Worse than a hindrance, it is a mortal hazard, a minefield taking a heavy toll of each and every new generation which we drive across it from the pristine ignorance of All Little Children to the goal of literacy and educability on the far side. Over a third of All Little Children can't keep their precarious balance on the narrow trail across, which seems so obvious and easy to us. They stumble and wander and fall and become victims of the minefield, many of them so psychologically wounded that even if they get back on the trail their progress is fearful and halting and their educability permanently impaired.

Bill Gates -- almost unique in the world -- has the resources, the power, the proven drive and initiative to achieve the transformation of America to Modular English. Why would he do it? Lesser people take their billions and buy a sports team and sink into a mindless oblivion of back-slapping and juvenile boosterism, round-the-clock cocktails and hors d'oeuvres. Even Bill Gates needs better advice than he has been getting -- God knows if the Pacific Northwest can absorb another environmental disaster of the magnitude of his so-called mansion. But if his existence isn't to compost in the same way as that of his super-wealthy contemporaries he must set a significant goal. Contrary to widespread opinion, medical research is not such a goal. There is no better idea than the process of aging and of the timely natural termination of peoples' lives. Sad as it may seem, increased longevity is *not* a valid goal. Curing AIDS, Alzheimer's, mental illness, drug addiction, solving all societies negative problems .... are like bailing a sinking Titanic. It's noble but hopeless. Some fraction of all people are going to suffer these horrible fates; others are going to get struck by lightning. Better Bill Gates should invest his immense personal resources for the benefit of the world's most precious resource -- All Little Children. He can't make it a perfectly safe place for them; he can't guarantee their health or their success or their prosperity or their behavior. What he can do is guarantee their *welcome*.

He can give them a language they can read and write and spell. All of them? No, not all of them. Some unfortunately but realistically cannot be reached. Many of them? Yes, absolutely. To oversimplify for the sake of a numerical answer: One third of All Little Children now have no problem with written English. These are not really our concern here, but they too will benefit tremendously from their automatic access to Modular English and can get on to idea-oriented studies. The second third -- to be crass and simplistic about it those with IQ's between 90 and 110 -- are our primary target and it is this group which benefits the most and *from which we will benefit the most*. Written language skills are not automatic for this group. They are forced to struggle and even experience failure. The less their learning ability, the more their frustration *and accompanying demoralization* as a result of the arbitrariness and inconsistency of the traditional written English language. This group has a perfectly adequate capacity to remember and to follow consistent instructions of considerable complexity; but they are brittle in their thought processes. They cannot sustain coherent thought and soon disintegrate under the bombardment of uncertainty and ambiguity, and actual deluge of chaotic and seemingly random choices which have to be made in traditional written English. The invalidation of their thought processes and the resulting *demoralization* of this large population of eminently educatable children is the principal harm done by traditional written English. The end of this destructive so-called education experience is the primary benefit of Modular English reform.

This could be Bill Gates second great heritage. Only he has the financial resources to correct the great fiasco of English spelling which baffles the learning abilities of so much of humankind; and he is one of the few who have the imagination, enterprise and spirit to join such a revolutionary cause at its very inception.

Sec XI.3: Finally! A Positive Media Blitzkrieg.

Oprah is chosen to lead the campaign on television and to publicize the merits and benefits of spelling reform.   Like Barbara Bush, Oprah Winfrey has the love and confidence of the vast majority of the people. She has a special access to women and young mothers whose near unanimous support and active participation is absolutely essential to a successful campaign for language reform. A favorable response must resound from the popular media and Oprah Winfrey's voice could dominate this response.

One of the great fears of mothers is that *their* children might get less than the best; that there might be a two-tier education system, and that they and theirs might get palmed-off with a 'dumbed-down' version. The result of course would be a split of society as in ancient Rome into Patricians and Plebians; or as in not-so-long-ago England into gentry and cockneys; where the unbridgeable class distinction was the permanent and obvious indelible stain of an accent. Recent experiments with a 'modern' approach to arithmetic have aroused just this cry: that the new way of adding (from left to right, like dollars first, then dimes, then pennies) is somehow dumbing-it-down. The opposite of course is the case. In fact, with generations of inflation why worry about the pennies at all; or the dimes. Just get the answer right to the nearest dollar. Nothing could be more realistic and sensible. But the fear of change is so universal and paranoia is so pervasive, that these obstructionist delusions must be addressed.

This paranoia is furthermore a manifestation of a complete misunderstanding of the nature of 'knowing' which identifies knowledge as the ability to regurgitate facts. We might as well be chanting hymns in some Tibetan dialect we can't translate. The more complicated the facts memorized, the more marvelous the 'knowledge' that is 'possessed'.   Therefore to simplify arithmetic -- or spelling -- is to devalue it as a mystifying achievement worthy of reward, recognition and -- most important of all -- of entitlement, place, preference, position, prestige. And the simpler it is made, and the more widespread

169

its mastery, the more it is taken for granted, the less entitled are all the old stockholders. It's like issuing a new paper currency without exchanging the old. When it does happen all those holding their old dollar bills will be left feeling somewhat empty handed. But not to worry! They *will* have to start -- but with the *huge* advantage of their previous literacy which makes the task almost trivial -- learning Modular English as a second written language. We should be pleased that the task is in fact almost trivial and can be mastered in less than a week by an already literate person. Praise God that it's trivial, because that is the *sole purpose* of the reform -- so that All Little Children in their millions can readily grasp reading, writing and spelling.

But here again we use a loaded word -- trivial. Hackles rise! Hostility flares. They are going to trivialize our language, our children's thoughts, our culture, our knowledge .... None of the above! On the contrary, we are going to give much easier and therefore earlier and more widespread access to learning with information *and idea* content and therefore to the much deeper conception of learning with understanding.

Oprah Winfrey has the ability and the power to persuade America that Modular English reform serves the best interests of *all* Americans. Oprah Winfrey's access to the hearts of all Americans gives the TV industry the opportunity to wage a proverbial Marshal Plan to repair some of the damage that traditional written English is wreaking on our children and has wreaked on our people. A successful campaign for Modular English reform would be one of the greatest public services ever performed, and comparable in its positive and lasting impact on the lives of All Little Children with the conquest of polio.

Liz Sulzberger Hollas is not a celebrity. She is a young mother of two, a lawyer, an athlete, and a distant relation of the *New York Times* Sulzbergers. Her role will be to manage relations with the traditional press and to ensure a sympathetic representation of Modular English reform in the nation's newspapers. What we would aim for in the campaign is sample news reports written in Modular English, perhaps culminating in a national day in which all major newspapers published their whole edition in Modular English. We can anticipate a deluge of hostile reaction from columnists and 'Letters' contributors. These must be handled patiently and with good humor by the press and be countered by reasoned arguments from sympathetic experts in such areas as psychology, linguistics, and pedagogy.

Michael Jordan brings to the cause his unrivaled persona and the absolutely hypnotic trance that he is able to cast over the elite power structure of corporate America. His power as an ambassador to sway corporate opinion and to get every major business and industrial and financial leader to sign on with the cause of language reform is absolutely essential. It is important that he make these contacts very early in the campaign -- probably, pending wiser counsel, before any other publicity -- in order to preempt any reflexive reactionary response from a group which one might anticipate being quite conservative. The reform campaign is going to be intrinsically political but not necessarily polarized along traditional liberal-conservative, Democrat-Republican lines. It would be Michael Jordan's mission to blunt any reactionary response and to get eminent conservatives to sign on for broad based and powerful bipartisan support. In summary, Michael Jordan's primary role is political. It must be his top priority to persuade CEO's and comparable power figures that their allegiance is appropriately owed to Modular English reform. Corporate funding and financial support -- although important -- are coincidental to this fundamental goal.

Bill Gates Sr. as director of the Gates Family Trust is in a directly powerful position to commit financial resources to the campaign. He also has other valuable attributes. His status gives him the credibility and access to reinforce Michael Jordan's ambassadorial role by his own follow-up corporate fund raising efforts. Another great role for Bill Gates Sr. would be as a liaison to the AARP. Their support in the campaign would be potent and mutually beneficial. If the AARP could be persuaded to take an outspoken role in favor of this issue, which is not directly related to their own self-interest but rather to that of their grandchildren, it would be envigorating for them, persuasive for us, and further ennoble their other political activities.

Secretary of Defense William Cohen, George Prescott Bush, and (soon-to-be ex-) President William Jefferson Clinton are put forward as liaison-cum-lobbyists for federal, state and local governments. Their skills and assets for these roles are compelling. The product they are selling is compelling also, and promises to release tremendous educational resources at the state and local level to be reinvested in the skills of the new technological age. President Clinton is a special case whose choice -- although perhaps obvious to many -- needs some explanation. In spite of his well-known shortcomings and transgressions, he is one of the great persuaders. We need to employ him in something more significant than the usual ex-president limbo of celebrity golf and corporate handouts. He is young enough for a significant second career and campaigning for language reform at the local level can employ his best skills to their fullest.

And finally we come to Secretary of State Madeline Albright. For a post-political career, she is ideally suited to be the nations surrogate Jewish mother which many of us sorely need. Whatever it is that Jewish mothers are supposed to do, the nation needs some of it now. We must do the right thing under threat that Madeline Albright will whither us with her disapproval.

And finally, finally don't forget former-UN Ambassador and soon-to-be former-Secretary of Energy Bill Richardson whose expertise at herding cats will be sorely taxed by having to organize and carry out a campaign with so many disparate groups united only by the thin thread of their unadmitted inability to spell.

Sec XI.4: New Business Opportunities.

Beginning immediately, we must publish new books and dictionaries in Modular English. The details of their versions of the new written language are not intended to be definitive -- the new language is non-unique and permissive and an on-going work-in-progress, remember. Microsoft's Encarta has the opportunity to lead the charge.

There will also be a great demand to republish selected old books in the new language. This is a marvelous challenge for computerized translation and online publication companies. The new phonetic Modular English should also facilitate computerized audio-reproductions of books for the blind. There is also a great new opportunity to write new textbooks in Modular English, and hopefully they will be user friendly, available online, and perhaps also in Free-Schools and Free-Universities on the internet.

Sec XI.5: Opening Salvos. The NYT Leads the Charge.

One of the great experiences in the whole reform adventure will be to rattle the cage of the self-proclaimed humanitarians of the liberal-intellectual elite. It is not at all obvious where they will take their stand on this issue. Can the effete intellectual snobs of the New Yorker stoop to support such a liberal-humanitarian down-and-dirty enterprise as rewriting their beautifully cultivated mastery of English? Will the columnists of the New York Times rally-round-the-flag of egalitarianism?

Surely William Safire will have something pithy to say at every step. He will be like the archeologists under threat of the Aswan Dam, trying to stave off the muddy waters and save what he can. Construct a time capsule of all your word-smithy treasures. And William Buckley? Surprise us, both William S. and William B. That's all we ask: Surprise us.

The New York Times could also surprise us by running one day a week in Modular English. Surely no one who reads the NYT needs the help of Modular English, but there are millions of little children out there who do need your help. And not just a passing glance, not fifteen minutes of fame. Join us in the heavy lifting; make this your cause, too. Put your corporate minds to the task of making your columns accessible to ten year old 4th graders. Not all the columns, of course. But the columns about dinosaurs and the ones about basketball. Win All Little Children over to reading your newspaper one story at a time by making them accessible in the Modular English language of our future.

Sec XI.6: A New Springtime for Humankind.

All Little Children will feel loved, and will be happy and able to run free, to sing and play and dance lightly in circles tossing rose petals in the air, and to spell and write well and to have voice at last; and we will all grow old joyfully, each Gregory Peck loving his own Audrey Hepburn.

The End

About The Author

Ian Duck was born and raised – with sisters Shirley and Marjorie and cousins Pamela, Peter and Penelope – on a sheep and cattle ranch in Central British Columbia; remembers with much nostalgia a fantasy childhood of ranch work, hunting and fur trapping; schooled up to the eighth grade in a one room log cabin with about ten others in all grades. Went to "town" for high school, "back east" for university, and "down to the States" for graduate school; and eventually to Houston, Texas as a Professor of Physics and Astronomy at Rice University. Married twice, father of Eric, Sarah and Lydia; grandfather of Ricky, Hunter, Laura and Caroline. An avid but inept tennis player and a compulsive reader.